Case Studies in School Leadership

W. Grant Hambright

UNIVERSITY PRESS OF AMERICA,® INC.
Dallas • Lanham • Boulder • New York • Oxford

Copyright © 2004 by
University Press of America,® Inc.
4501 Forbes Boulevard
Suite 200
Lanham, Maryland 20706
UPA Acquisitions Department (301) 459-3366

PO Box 317
Oxford
OX2 9RU, UK

All rights reserved
Printed in the United States of America
British Library Cataloging in Publication Information Available

Library of Congress Control Number: 2004109354
ISBN 0-7618-2800-1 (paperback : alk. ppr.)

∞™ The paper used in this publication meets the minimum
requirements of American National Standard for Information
Sciences—Permanence of Paper for Printed Library Materials,
ANSI Z39.48—1992

Contents

CASES A through B

Accommodating Special Needs Students	1
Accommodating Supplemental Instruction	2
Addressing a Leaderless Campus	3
Addressing Cafeteria Concerns	4
Addressing Curriculum Confusion	6
Addressing Drug Problems	8
Addressing Outside Recess Parameters	9
Addressing Secondary-Level Reading Problems	10
Adopting a New Curricular Program	11
Aligning District and Campus Personnel Roles	12
Appraising a Family Member	14
Assessing Building Climate	15
Assessing Current Student Tardy Policies	17
Assessing Non-Custodial Parents' Rights	18
Assessing School Office Decorum	19
Assessing the Legal Status of Student Teachers	21
Assigning Homework	22
Assigning Students to Achievement Groups	23
Assuring School Personnel Safety	25

Attending Both Public and Private School Classes — 26
Attending to Gifted Students' Needs — 27
Banning Cell Phones in School — 28

CASES C through D

Centralizing School Supplies — 29
Changing from Teaching to Administrative Duties — 30
Cheating on the Test — 32
Collecting Funds for Social Concerns — 34
Communicating Through Proper Channels — 35
Comparing Students' Efforts During a Parent-Teacher Conference — 37
Compiling a Substitute Teachers' Handbook — 39
Configuring Central Office Personnel Needs — 40
Confronting an Influential Booster Group — 42
Considering a Mandatory Drug Testing Program — 44
Considering a New Budgeting Approach — 46
Controlling Library Censorship — 47
Controlling the Release of Students from School — 48
Controlling Violence in a Special Education Classroom — 49
Dealing With an Ineffective Principal — 50
Defending Against Discrimination Accusations — 51
Determining Board Members' Political Agendas — 52
Determining Classified Personnel Job Descriptions — 53
Determining Homework Accountability — 54
Determining Teacher Effectiveness — 55
Developing a Safety Program — 56
Developing Classroom Management Expectations — 57
Developing Special Educational Job Descriptions — 58
Disclosing Sensitive Issues — 59

Dismissing an Administrator	60
Displaying Inappropriate Public Behavior	61
Dueling Supervisory Authorities	63

CASES E through I

Eliminating Underclassman Hazing	64
Enacting a Weapons Zero-Tolerance Policy	66
Evaluating School Supply Procedures	68
Evaluating Support Staff Performance	69
Evaluating Teaching Effectiveness through Classroom Observations	70
Extending Special Favors to School Board Members	71
Grooming Standards for Student Teachers	72
Grouping Grade Levels within a School District	74
Guarding Against Possible HIV Contamination	76
Handling a Crisis Situation	77
Handling a Disruptive Student	78
Handling a Split P.T.O.	79
Handling Common Transportation Problems	81
Handling Complaints about Maintenance Personnel	82
Handling Student Discipline Problems	83
Handling the Unauthorized Use of School Facilities	85
Harassing a Teacher: The Principal's Perspective	86
Harassing a Teacher: The Teacher's Perspective	88
Having Good Intentions but Setting a Bad Example	90
Hiring a New Building Principal	92
Honoring a School Board Directive	93
Impeding the School's Custodial Services	94
Implementing a New Leadership Style	95
Improving Campus Staff Teamwork	96

Improving Custodial Services	97
Improving Special Needs Students' Achievement Levels	98
Improving Student Attendance	99
Increasing Public Support of Education	100
Initiating Supervisory Functions	101

CASES L through P

Leaving a Special Education Classroom Unattended	102
Locating a Missing Child	103
Maintaining Harmony Among Faculty	104
Making Pupil Assignment Decisions	106
Managing Maintenance Personnel	107
Mandating School Uniforms	108
Mentoring New Teachers	109
Merging Two Rival Schools	110
Minimizing Teaching Interruptions	111
Minimizing the Effects of a Transient Student Population	112
Missing Curriculum Guides	113
Monitoring Locker Rooms	115
Observing Student-Initiated Segregation	116
Overemphasizing High School Football	117
Planning Effective Faculty Meetings	118
Pledging to the American Flag	120
Praying at Football Games	212
Preparing an Integrated Instructional Unit	122
Preparing for Parent-Teacher Conferences	123
Preventing Plagiarism	125
Preventing Potential Internet Abuse	127

Preventing School Personnel From Using Others' Personal Materials	129
Prioritizing School Administrator Professional Development Activities	130
Prioritizing Teacher Requests	132
Promoting a Proposed Administrator Evaluation System	133
Protecting Our Children	134

CASES R through U

Rating Teachers on the Internet	135
Reducing the Cost of Education	137
Regulating Participation in Extracurricular Activities	138
Removing a Bad Reputation	140
Requiring School District Residency	142
Requiring Teachers to Perform Additional Duties	143
Resolving Personality Conflicts	144
Respecting the Assistant Principal	145
Respecting the Confidentiality of Special Needs Students	146
Revamping a Dysfunctional Grade-Level Team	148
Revamping High School Graduation Ceremonies	149
Reviewing an Open Campus Policy	150
Reviewing the Treasurer's Files	152
Revising a Teacher Sick Leave Policy	153
Revising Teacher Employment Applications	154
Revising Teacher Observation Criteria	156
Revising Teacher Transfer Policies	157
Selecting High School Cheerleaders	158
Selecting New Textbooks	159
Treating Student Athletes Equally	160
Using School Facilities by Community Groups	162

Index (By People Involved) 163
Index (By Sites) 173
Index (By Topic) 177

Introduction

The purpose of this book is to provide discussion-starters through case studies for educational administration and leadership classes. "While traditional methods may be effective in covering many aspects of educational leadership, the case study method offers an interesting alternative" (Diamantes & Ovington, 2003, p. 465). First used in legal coursework, the case study method has gained acceptance by many examining the principles of business administration (Merseth, 1991) and more recently the general topics in the field of education (Tillman, 1995). Case studies provide students opportunities to: link theoretical concepts to practical field experiences; refine critical thinking, decision-making, and problem solving skills; and, utilize reflective techniques within a leadership context (Kolwaski, 2001). According to Merseth, two other advantages of case method usage include involving students in their own learning and promoting community building within an educational setting.

These posed problems in education are written with case study methodology in mind. As in many case study approaches, incomplete narratives or scenarios are presented accompanied by thought provoking or discussion stimulating questions. This is done to facilitate use of the problem descriptions with or without prior reading assignments and study. One teaching strategy is to divide classes into small discussion groups (four to five students) who read the problems, brainstorm for solutions, and then present their collaborative findings to the whole class. A similarly successful approach uses the scenarios as focused discussion pieces within an online discussion group context.

The problems presented here may be used in conjunction with various traditional texts or serve as bases for group discussion covering various educational leadership and administration concepts. The cases within this text, by design, vary in length and degree of background specificity. These factors facilitate flexibility in their use by instructors. The cases in this text could be useful in the following types of educational leadership and administration courses:

Introduction to Educational Administration	School Housing and Facilities
School Finance	School Law
Personnel Administration	The Principalship
Instructional Supervision	School Community Relations
The Superintendency	Ethics and Politics in Education
Special Services Administration	
Research for the Instructional Leader	

Case titles typically indicate the case's primary focus; however, many cases have multiple embedded foci. Accompanying indices detail the potential discussion topics, people involved, and settings presented. As in most case study materials, there is seldom one "right" answer to the posed questions.

Most educational leadership and administration classes enroll experienced teachers, and in some cases inexperienced individuals from fields outside of education, who are preparing for various leadership positions. These multiple perspectives are invaluable in the problem-solving and decision-making processes highlighted in classroom and online discussions. In many instances the collective wisdom of the class provides immediate solutions to the stated problems while in other ill-structured situations there may appear to be no solution at all. With these concerns in mind, the following case studies and questions are offered as useful tools for students preparing for educational leadership and administration positions.

REFERENCES

Diamantes, Thomas, and June Ovington. "Storytelling: Using a Case Method Approach in Administrator Preparation Programs." *Education 1233*. (Spring, 2003): 465–469.

Kowalski, T. *Case Studies on Educational Administration*. 3d ed. New York: Longman 2001.

Merseth, K.K. *A Case for Cases in Teacher Education*. American Association for Colleges for Teacher Education: Washington, D.C., 1991.

Tillman, B.A. "Reflection on Case Method Teaching." *Action in Teacher Education* 16, no.1 (1995): 1–8.

Accommodating Special Needs Students

Case

Golden Valley School District's central office recently notified elementary principal, Grace Gordon, that additional students have been assigned to her building. Grandview Elementary School will house a newly formed Educationally Mentally Handicapped (EMH) class, as there is a sufficient amount of identified students and the school has a couple of vacant classrooms. The students will arrive in two weeks, yet the newly hired and qualified teacher, Heather Henderson, reports on duty tomorrow.

Discussion

1. What planning needs to take place? List all plans.
2. Should Ms. Gordon provide an induction program for the new teacher? Why or why not?
3. What considerations need to be made regarding these special education students?

Accommodating Supplemental Instruction

Case

Dan Dearborn, principal at Bluebird Elementary School, feels fortunate to have a full-time school nurse assigned to his campus. Most of the district's schools have only part-time nurses, and a few have no nurse at all. Dr. Dearborn assigns Bluebird's nurse, Betty Brown, to visit classes to present health and wellness information supplementing various curricula throughout the building. When Betty approaches some teachers with this idea, they kindly schedule convenient times and discuss various topics that need reinforcing. However, this warm reception is not universal. Several teachers refuse Ms. Brown's offer. These teachers imply that her talks will only rehash previously discussed content. They further contend that unless the material is on the state-mandated standardized test, they simply do not the time for it. Ms. Brown is following Dr. Dearborn's request, and she is persistent with her offers. Several nay-saying teachers report that they are tired of being harassed.

Discussion

1. How can Dr. Dearborn gain acceptance of Nurse Brown's requests by the teachers?
2. Is Dr. Dearborn wrong in trying to supplement regular instruction by bringing in a specialist? Why or why not?
3. How can supplemental programs be implemented? Describe a viable plan.
4. How much of the problem can be attributed to the individual personalities of the key players?

Addressing a Leaderless Campus

Case

Marianne Michelson begins her last year as Cameron City High School's principal on a rough note. She becomes quite ill, and ultimately, needs surgery. Her two assistant principals continue doing their assigned duties as well as handle all of Ms. Michelson's responsibilities. The CCHS staff feels like the campus' mission and goals are "on hold" until Marianne returns.

After recovering from surgery for several weeks, Ms. Michelson returns, but on a significantly reduced work schedule. Unfortunately, Marianne's recovery is severely slowed with recurring illnesses, and the short stays at school become routine. After three months of this work pattern, several school board members and district administrators concede that Ms. Michelson's inconsistent leadership adversely affects the CCHS programs, staff, and students. The district superintendent, Randy Reed, feels compelled to address this situation within the next few weeks.

Discussion

1. Make a list of steps Mr. Reed could take in addressing this problem.
2. List three alternatives to the plan detailed in Question 1.
3. There are many reasons for taking action in the scenario given. Reviewing the following list, discuss how they are affected by this situation: (a) students; (b) teachers; (c) support staff; (d) parents; (e) board of education; (f) district administrators; and, (g) community members
4. Describe how those groups mentioned in Question 3 could be affected by Mr. Reed's action plan.

Addressing Cafeteria Concerns

Case

Mary McGregor, the school cafeteria manager at Montgomery Middle School, schedules an appointment with building principal, Ron Ralston, regarding ongoing cafeteria concerns. Upon entering the office, Mary hands Ron a typed list. He notes that the paper is shaking as he takes it from Mary's firm grasp. The initial concerns are constant student complaints about food choices and its quality. Ron smiles to himself as he personally agrees with the first two points, but he continues to scan the list as Mary's demeanor indicates she is probably at her wit's end. Student rudeness and noisiness are the next concerns followed by students' unwillingness to clean up messes and return their trays when they finish eating. Mary's list also claims that teachers are no help with these problems as they generally avoid the cafeteria during their lunch breaks.

Mr. Ralston looks up from the list as Ms. McGregor says, "I follow the district recommendations for menu planning. I do the best with what I have to work with. I strive to provide quality wholesome meals every day, but lately it's been a challenge."

Ron nods his head in agreement and asks Mary, "What, if any, effects are we feeling from the new shopping plaza's food court down the street?"

"Oh, those new fast food places are throwing my numbers way off. Students claim they are going to eat in the cafeteria when the morning lunch count is taken, but then they leave campus and go eat at the plaza," claims Ms. McGregor.

Mr. Ralston realizes now that the open campus policy may need to be revisited, and jots down this additional note at the bottom of the list. As he finishes his writing, Ms. McGregor adds, "You would think that having an assistant principal supervising in the cafeteria would help curb some of the bad student behaviors, but Mr. Adams doesn't seem to ever notice anything unless it's printed in the newspaper's sport section." Mr. Ralston sighs and promptly scribbles another note at the bottom of the typed list.

Discussion

1. What can be done to verify Ms. McGregor's report?
2. Does this mean that Mr. Ralston will have to monitor the lunchroom from now on? Why or why not?
3. Should the students be allowed to eat lunch off-campus? Why or why not?
4. Outline some suggested strategies for improving this situation.
5. Who should have a part in the solution and how will they participate?

Addressing Curriculum Confusion

Case

Sandy Shore, a new second grade teacher at Beachside Elementary School, is confused. It's November, and she just attended a meeting with all of the kindergarten through fourth grade teachers. The main agenda item was to discuss the Christmas Around the World Unit that had traditionally been taught in all grade levels for at least the past fifteen years or at least that was according to one of the third grade teachers, fifteen-year veteran, Betty Brookshire. Betty quickly organized the agenda, emailed it to the building teachers earlier in the day, and started the after school meeting by stating, "We've had some personnel changes during the past couple years, and I think we need to re-evaluate how we go about teaching this unit."

"I don't know that we should be teaching a religious concept in our public school anyway. Furthermore, our recent influx of students from various ethnic and cultural backgrounds makes me tend to not want to dwell on a potentially sensitive issue such as Christmas," stated one first grade teacher. That brought about a flurry of side conversations, until Betty regained the teachers' attention by saying, "We won't go there. I see your point, but we're not here to decide whether we teach the unit or not. We're here to determine how it's going to be taught."

"I won't have time to cover the material in the Social Studies textbook, if we add this unit. Anyway, I just barely get through the necessary content prior to our students taking their achievement tests in mid-March," snapped fourth grade teacher, Martha Middleton. "Hear, hear!" shouted another fourth grade teacher. "My second grade textbook already has a unit dealing with various holiday celebrations around the world, so this unit Betty is talking about will simply enhance the textbook topics," replied Lori Langston. The two other second grade teachers shook their heads in agreement with Ms. Langston's comments. "Lori, what social studies textbooks are you talking about?" queries Ms. Shore.

This question brought an eerie pall to the normally chatty atmosphere. Except for the newcomer, Ms. Shore, the second grade teachers were Beachside Elementary faculty for the past five years or more. These three teachers exchanged uncomfortable glances with each other, as well as across the room with other colleagues. "Oh, we're sorry, Sandy. Didn't you know there were social studies texts in the storeroom down the hall from our classrooms?" From this point onward, Sandy did not pay attention to the remainder of the meeting's business, because she kept wondering about what other curricular items about which she was uninformed.

Discussion

1. Who could Ms. Shore ask about the curricular items of which she should be aware?
2. What are some of the problems embedded in this scenario? Explain your answers.
3. Should the teachers be more sensitive to their students' diversity? Why or why not?

Addressing Drug Problems

Case

Retirement cannot happen soon enough for Monroeville High School principal, Cam Cannon. At a recent meeting, the superintendent indicates he is getting phone calls from MHS parents concerned about an alleged drug problem. Although Cam never knew of a confirmed drug problem, he knew that he had recently fielded several phone calls as well from alarmed parents about this same issue. The parents claim their children are frightened. Teachers report that they suspect students store marijuana and LSD in their lockers. Some faculty members contend students sell the illegal substances from within the school building.

As a first step toward addressing this major issue, Mr. Cannon conducts an informal discussion with school staff and receives the following suggestions: (a) inform police officials about the problem and ask for their assistance; (b) determine if police can place undercover police officers in the school as students; (c) conduct locker searches to confiscate drugs and related paraphernalia; (d) request police drug-sniffing dogs check all school lockers; (e) request police drug-sniffing dogs walk up and down classroom aisles while students sit at their desks; (f) demand that students submit to strip searches if drug-sniffing dogs identify them as suspects; (g) search suspicious vehicles in the parking lot including students and staff; (h) place a "hot tips" box in the main hall where anonymous notes can be placed revealing suspected drug users and dealers; and, (i) mandate that drug users and/or dealers be given immediate expulsion, without a hearing, if it is determined that they are guilty.

Discussion

1. Which rules should be implemented? Why?
2. Which rules should not be implemented? Why?
3. Suggest other strategies for addressing the problem.

Addressing Outside Recess Parameters

Case

Billie Brown is the principal at Hammond Elementary School, a school located in the Midwest. As usual, each winter brings a variety of weather conditions and temperatures between 0° to 60°F. Throughout much of February, temperatures have been fairly consistent, ranging from 20° to 25°F each school day. Wind chill has not been noticeable. Ms. Brown's unwritten policy is that students have outdoor recess as long is there is no ice, sleet, or rain, and the temperature is at least 20°F or above. Several parents have called the school and asked that their children remain indoors during the month. Reasons for this varied, but mainly the concern was air temperature.

Discussion

1. Based on the unwritten policy that she uses to guide her judgment concerning outdoor recess, what should Billie Brown tell the parents that have requested their children stay indoors?
2. What are the ramifications of this issue?
3. Are their alternatives to the parents' requests? Explain your answer.
4. Who could Billie Brown involve in making decisions about parameters for outdoor recess?

Addressing Secondary-Level Reading Problems

Case

Walter Winslow is the newly appointed principal at Northside High School. He and four new teachers, Angela Atkins, Bruce Bellows, Connie Christian, and David Dennison were hired by the district's school board to help boost academic scores at this school. The teaching quartet represented a mixture of veteran educators who were considered to be outstanding instructors in their respective areas of mathematics, social studies, science, and language arts.

Soon after the onset of school, these four teachers and Walter assess their initial impressions of student work thus far. Walter had Angela, Bruce, Connie, and David list the top three academic weaknesses of their students. Consensus indicated that most students were poor readers and could be labeled as "less than mediocre." These reading deficiencies, the teachers contend, interfere with academic progress in almost every academic area. Mr. Winslow brings the matter to Felice Franklin's attention. She is the supervisor of secondary instruction and she claims that she has not previously heard of any such problem. Felice frankly doubts the students' reading abilities are any lower in this high school than any of the district's other high schools.

Discussion

1. What can be done to address this problem?
2. If you were a person involved in this case, what techniques would you use to improve reading instruction?
3. Are we justified in concluding that reading is poorly taught in the schools in the city? Why or why not?
4. What should be done to acquaint the grade school teachers with the problem?
5. To what extent, if any, would you substitute work-type reading for literature in the high school classes?
6. Can remedial reading be taught by high schools? Who is best qualified to teach this?

Adopting a New Curricular Program

Case

Rosalyn Reynolds, the curriculum supervisor at Lancaster Schools, is concerned about the newly adopted mathematics curriculum for Grades K–5. The district has spent a considerable amount of time and money investigating various programs, and Math For Everyday (MFE) appealed to her as well as many of the teachers. This spiral curriculum approach consistently revisits previously discussed and mastered concepts and skills while simultaneously introducing newer, more advanced content.

The MFE proponents like the program because math skills are not taught in discrete units but are constantly reviewed in relation with other skills. Other teachers and some administrators embrace their former approach where skills were not blended as being a better curriculum, especially for struggling students. One fourth grade teacher expressed this sentiment, "I think that MFE is an excellent math program; however, I don't know if the parents will understand or appreciate that we are teaching students there are multiple ways of solving math problems." After hearing this statement, Dr. Reynolds thinks about what steps to take next.

Discussion

1. Has Dr. Reynolds and the MFE proponents "sold" all of the educational community on the new math program? Explain your answer.
2. Should Dr. Reynolds strive for a total buy-in of the MFE program before it is implemented? Why or why not?
3. What strategies could be employed to help alleviate the concern expressed by the fourth grade teacher?

Aligning District and Campus Personnel Roles

Case

The superintendent of Pleasant Valley Schools, Jean Johnston, notices conflicts occurring between campus administrators and the central office personnel in this small school district. Two recent events readily come to mind. First, Mark Mulligan, the district's personnel director, wants to assign teachers to the various schools based on human resources management guidelines while the district's principals want a voice in all personnel placements. For example, Mr. Mulligan recently opted to remove a teacher from Eaglecrest Elementary because her teaching credentials matched a teaching vacancy at Forestdale Middle School. This teacher was very upset because her assignment at Eaglecrest was an ideal one considering her Autistic son attends school there. The teacher was threatening to resign because she could not disrupt her son's educational routine by leaving him at Eaglecrest, and the building principal was incensed that he would have to find an elementary music teacher so close to the beginning of the school year. Ms. Johnston intervened to prevent the loss of an excellent teacher and to calm both the agitated principal and the now irate personnel manager.

Another recent incident involved Ann Applebury, the district's business manager, and some the district's principals. Ms. Applebury has sole responsibility for developing campus- and district-level budgets. Some campus principals want to shift funds from one category to another to meet their campus needs. For example, two campus principals want to move funds from the capital outlay category to a professional development area because there is a greater need for funding in the latter area due to low test score results. Ms. Applebury claims that moving funds at this juncture in the fiscal year is impossible and denies the principals' requests. The campus principals contend their campus needs are not being addressed and discuss this matter with Ms. Johnston. The superintendent intervenes and asks the business manager to find funds for these essential instructional needs.

With both of these incidents on her mind, Jean searches the central office files for an organizational chart. She hopes that by finding the graphic, she can help prevent future discord between central office staff and campus level administration. Jean is disheartened as the most current copy she locates is fifteen years old and it does not adequately match the current organizational structures.

Discussion

1. Ideally, what should an organizational chart look like? Explain your response.
2. Is the chart, or lack thereof, the real issue here? Why or why not?
3. What can Superintendent Johnston do to improve the relationship between the levels of school administration?

Appraising a Family Member

Case

Anita Reyes, a veteran teacher at River Road High School, eagerly awaits today's classroom observation by the new high school principal. Her freshman-level English students are an exceptionally eager group this year, and she spent weeks preparing this unit on American authors. During her preparation period she fine-tuned her PowerPoint presentation, double-checked the VCR's videotape, and recounted the printed handouts. Everything appears to be ready for today's special introductory lesson.

Previous classroom observations indicate that Ms. Reyes is one of the building's outstanding teachers, but the weight of today's outcome has her more anxious than usual. This assessment of her teaching abilities will be pivotal in deciding whether or not she obtains tenure. Gaining tenure in this school district means an annual pay increase of $7,000. Another factor adding to her stress is, that for the first time in her teaching career, her husband is the building administrator observing her. Today's observation also marks the initial teacher observation in his new administrative role, and he too, is anxious about this event.

Discussion

1. Is there an ethical dilemma present in this case? Why or why not?
2. What would you do if you were the high school principal? Explain your answer.
3. What resources need to be accessed in order to guide their decision-making?

Assessing Building Climate

Case

Lana Lindley was recently assigned to be the new principal at Rolling Hills Elementary School. After looking through personnel records and visiting with the school office staff, she learns there is very little teacher turnover at this K–5 school. Three teacher resignations last year and two retirements a couple of years ago are the largest personnel fluctuations the campus experienced within the past decade. The teachers pride themselves in their service to the school and district. According to one office assistant, most veteran teachers literally glow as they recount the number of principals they outlast.

Within the past several weeks, Lana informally chats with several teachers to get their perceptions of how problem situations were handled in the past. Lana gathers that most teachers thought that problems were handled quite well, and that there was little or no reason to change those procedures. The veteran teachers made it clear to Lana that they expected the new teachers to quickly "earn their stripes" by adopting the building's traditional approaches just like everyone else has done over the years.

The five newest teachers have been exposed to this thinking and request a meeting with Lana. These teachers were assigned to Rolling Hills after a lengthy, competitive process, as many new teachers applied for these infrequent openings at this highly regarded elementary school. Ms. Lindley considers these newcomers as some of the best teachers in the district. In their meeting, they open up about the flack they catch from the veteran teachers when suggesting alternative ways of teaching and managing students. Ms. Lindley adds the new teachers' concerns to the bulk of parent complaints that also center on the "old-timers'" attitudes. Collectively, the new teachers and parents feel that the veteran teachers are too set in their ways and are simply displaying their desire to be the ones in charge.

Discussion

1. From your perspective, this case study highlights what issue(s)? What action(s) should be taken first?
2. Is one viewpoint more "right" than another? Why or why not?
3. Should Ms. Lindley ask for help from central office? Why or why not?
4. How could Ms. Lindley handle the new teachers? Parents?
5. How should Ms. Lindley approach the "old-timers"? Are they united in their stand? Is this important?

Assessing Current Student Tardy Policies

Case

One of the assistant principal duties for Trevor Truman is handling student discipline problems. Student tardiness is a recurring problem at Madison High School. Teachers send all late arriving students to the office to obtain a tardy slip before allowing them admission to class. A student accumulating three tardies within a term must serve a teacher-monitored detention hall before or after school hours. Failing to attend a detention hall results in an automatic referral to a mandatory three-hour Saturday school supervised by the assistant principal.

Teachers claim that the current tardy policy punishes the teachers by creating a distraction at the beginning of each class, and that the detention hall time is a waste of their time. Mr. Truman contends that he is drowning in a sea of tardy slips and notices that students are not attending their assigned detention halls. Trevor is equally frustrated by the poorly attended Saturday school sessions that ultimately result with him losing a part of his weekend. Meanwhile, student tardiness remains an ongoing problem.

Discussion

1. What are some viable policy options for this campus to consider towards curtailing the problems with student tardiness?
2. Who do you assess to be ultimately responsible for the tardy problems? Why?
3. Should tardies be considered a disciplinary offense? Explain.
4. Is the amount of time spent dealing with the administration of the tardy policy by various campus personnel worth it? Justify your response.

Assessing Non-Custodial Parents' Rights

Case

It is 10:35 A.M. on Monday morning at Bliss Elementary School. Sue Stratford, the building principal, is attending a meeting in the central office, which is located 15 minutes from the school. Melissa Melcher, a student, is in the gym with the other third graders in her class as her biological father enters the school building.

Mike Melcher goes directly to Melissa's classroom. Teri Tomlinson and her teaching assistant are the only people in the classroom when the Mr. Melcher arrives.

Teri and the office personnel are aware that Mike does not have custodial rights.

Upon arriving in Ms. Tomlinson's room, Mr. Melcher appears irate and is acting very deranged. He informs Teri that he is taking his daughter with him now, and he demands to be told where Melissa is. At this same time, the physical education teacher is coming down the hallway with Ms. Tomlinson's third grade class.

Discussion

1. How does Teri Tomlinson begin to handle this potentially volatile situation?
2. After her attempt to communicate with the father and dispel his wishes to remove his daughter from the school, Teri finds he is adamant about taking her immediately. What is her next step?
3. Should Teri Tomlinson directly involve the teaching assistant and the physical education teacher with this issue? If yes, how? If no, why not?
4. What is Teri Tomlinson's legal responsibility, if any, in personally addressing this confrontation?

Assessing School Office Decorum

Case

As the new principal for Rockdale High School, Ron Randolph evaluates the merits and pitfalls of past practices within his new school's office setting. According to the office secretary, adult employees and student office workers use the following rules:

All school office personnel will:

- treat every visitor, teacher, and student with courtesy and respect;
- wear a nametag;
- conduct office business in the strictest confidence;
- attend to the manner and tone of verbal communication (for example, face-to-face and telephone conversation);
- attend to the manner and tone of written communication (for example, memos and emails); and,
- seek to help out others with office tasks.

Adult school office personnel will:

- leave word with the secretary as to his/her destination when he/she leaves the office for more than ten minutes;
- assign student assistants routine tasks that are not sensitive in nature;
- monitor the student assistants' actions when the students are idle; and,
- discourage visitors, teachers, and/or students from loitering or engaging in idle chitchat in the office.

Discussion

1. If you were Ron Randolph, how would you assess the present office rules? Explain your answer(s).

2. Based on the rules above, is there a need for additional or fewer rules to manage an effective and professional school office? If more are needed, then detail those additions. If fewer are warranted, pinpoint which one(s) and justify their elimination.
3. Which rules are commonly violated in school offices? Describe specific incidents.

Assessing the Legal Status of Student Teachers

Case

Denny Douglas asks his student teacher, Evan Engleton, to instruct his 8th grade science class in his absence while he temporarily leaves the building to take care of a banking matter. Mr. Douglas further suggests that perhaps Evan serve as a substitute teacher on days when he is completely absent from school. Evan agrees to his host teacher's request and suggestion. Mr. Engleton looks forward to these experiences.

Discussion

1. Should Evan Engleton be permitted to do these actions? Why or why not?
2. Who can be helpful in determining if these actions should be allowed?

Assigning Homework

Case

While watching students leave Waters Elementary School, Principal Dennis Duncan, notes the relatively small number of students carrying books home. Mr. Duncan gets the attention of a fourth grade student, Billy Benton, and asks him, "Billy, why aren't you taking home any books? " Billy responds, "Mr. Duncan, I don't have any homework. I finished all my work in class."

Mr. Duncan also queries several other students, who give very similar answers. Recent conversations with parents reveal that they also question why books seldom come home. Their children similarly report that their teachers provide ample class time for homework completion. The parents report that they do not feel like they know what is going on with their children's education if their children do not have homework.

Discussion

1. What should Mr. Duncan do?
2. Is it really necessary for students to have homework?
3. How should Mr. Duncan approach the faculty with this situation? Describe a couple of different tactics he could take.
4. Will parents have to be included in implementing a solution? Why or why not?

Assigning Students to Achievement Groups

Case

Grace Graham, the Floyd City Schools' curriculum director, is concerned about an intermediate school's instructional grouping practices. Each grade level's departmentalized fourth, fifth, and sixth grade teachers develop a manner of grouping students for instructional purposes. The current practice has teachers assigning students to one of five (red, blue, yellow, orange, or green) ability-based groups according to the students' fourth grade criterion-referenced test results. The red group mastered all the test objectives, the green group mastered very few to none of the test objectives, and the remaining three groups mastered various percentages of the test objectives.

Dr. Graham initially perceived these procedures as viable means for meeting the students' instructional needs until she learned two facts: (1) the students are assigned to their respective group based solely on their reading subtest mastery level; and, (2) the students remain in their assigned group throughout the instructional day. The teachers informed the curriculum director that students could be moved from one group to another if the teachers determined a student's placement was too advanced or too remedial to meet an individual student's academic needs.

Discussion

1. Why is Dr. Graham concerned about such student grouping practices? Explain.
2. Describe some alternative instructional grouping schemes for this grade level.
3. Who should be involved in determining this grade level's new grouping plan? Consider the following: (a) the curriculum director; (b) 4th, 5th,

and 6th grade teachers; (c) 4th, 5th, and 6th grade parents; (d) the campus principal; and, (e) an ad hoc committee comprised of each of these groups.
4. What are some potential problems associated with the current instructional grouping plan if it remains unchanged?

Assuring School Personnel Safety

Case

Margaret Miller, the school secretary, reports to the principal, Anne Ashwood, that Donna Dunsford just left the office in tears after receiving a telephone call. Ms. Dunsford told Margaret that her ex-husband is "on the way" to school to confront her and continue their ongoing dispute face-to-face. Margaret is visibly shaken as she relays this message to Ms. Ashwood.

Discussion

1. What actions are required?
2. Who should be notified about the occurrence?
3. Do these types of situations influence others as well? How?
4. Should a policy be in place for handling these types of concerns?

Attending Both Public and Private School Classes

Case

Joanna Jergins' past schooling has been in a parochial elementary school for the past eight years. The Jergins' three other daughters go to the same school. They realize that St. Elizabeth's High School's tuition is higher, and make the difficult decision to have Joanna attend the local public high school, Fort Jackson High. The Jergins want Joanna to continue having some sort of religious training, so they approach Superintendent Ian Innskeep about the possibility of Joanna attending two one-half hour religious classes a week at St. Elizabeth's. They remind Mr. Innskeep about the close proximity, three blocks, of the parochial school to Fort Jackson High School.

Discussion

1. Should Superintendent Innskeep grant this request? Why or why not?
2. Would granting such a request violate the intent of an attendance law? Explain your answer.
3. Does this violate the church-state separation concept? Why or why not?

Attending to Gifted Students' Needs

Case

The Valley View, a local newspaper, has recently been inundated with editorials concerning how much attention school district personnel expend to special education students. Comments in these letters indicate that gifted students' needs go unheeded due to the inordinate demands of the educationally challenged children. School officials' rebuttal letters assert that federal law dictates the amount of services rendered to the special education students. Gifted and talented students' parents decry that the disparity of academic services rendered is unfair. Teachers are beginning to join this group's bandwagon as they see the need for initiating gifted and talented classes.

Discussion

1. What approaches would you suggest the school district take in handling the needs of gifted students?
2. Should a gifted and talented program be established? Why?
3. How can the district determine which students should be included in this group?
4. Which teachers should be involved in this program? Why?
5. Are there any other problems in this scenario other than attending to the academic needs of the gifted students?

Banning Cell Phones in School

Case

The Twin Lakes School District Board of Education recently adopts a policy banning students from possessing cell phones, pagers, and portable music devices during school hours. The board contends these electronic devices potentially distract students and teachers from successfully fulfilling their designated duties. Several teacher groups, the district's police force, and various administrators assert that these gadgets pose as potential theft targets and could be used for communication channels supporting illegal activities such as drug sales, prostitution, illicit photography, and terrorism further support the school board's stance.

The Twin Lakes High School Student Council president, Kyle Kincaid, notifies the district superintendent, Nowell Norton, his desire for time at the next school board meeting. Kyle and the student council consider the new policy infringes on their 1st Amendment rights. They also rebut the communication channel point by citing that in the Columbine High School and World Trade Center tragedies electronic devices, such as those banned by the board, served as lifelines to families and external safety officials. These high school students plan to serve the school board with a petition signed by three fourths of the student body requesting this policy be reconsidered.

Discussion

1. How should Nowell Norton handle Kyle Kincaid's request?
2. Has the Twin Lakes school board made a valid policy? Why or why not?
3. Has the Twin Lakes High School Student Council made a reasonable argument against the electronic devices ban? Explain your answer.
4. Should Nowell Norton assemble an ad hoc committee to look into this issue? Why or why not? If yes, who should serve on this committee?
5. Is there a reasonable compromise between the two stances depicted in this case? Explain your reasoning.

Centralizing School Supplies

Case

Until recently, Carlton Criswell, a supervisor in the Bloomington United School District's central office, had not given much thought to the processes utilized for supplying the schools with essential materials. He assumed that the current method of schools placing orders and the district obtaining the wanted items worked reasonably well. A new colleague in the central office informed Carlton that in her former district they used a "standard supply list." This means that the district develops lists of materials that all the district buildings use. By buying the listed items in bulk, the district subsequently saves money. Mr. Criswell likes the way this processes sounds, and starts working on a proposal. He determines that most of the district's supply expenditures fall into the following categories: (a) Instructional Supplies, (b) Computers/Software; (c) Office Supplies; and, (d) Custodial/Cleaning Supplies.

Discussion

1. Where should Mr. Criswell go from here in developing the standard supply lists?
2. Who should be involved in developing the contents of each list? Explain your answer.
3. How could Mr. Criswell organize this project?
4. Start a list for each of the four areas and see how many items emerge.

Changing from Teaching to Administrative Duties

Case

An eerie hush falls over the usual clamor in the teachers' lounge. The usual crowd for this time of day awkwardly assumes various temporary tasks upon Sheryl Shannon's entrance. Ms. Ferrell leafs through a magazine, Mr. Dawson clears the table of coffee paraphernalia, and Ms. Hill grades a stack of student papers. Sheryl knows these impromptu actions are not typically portions of this grouping's repertoire. For the previous five years, Ms. Shannon was a part of what had become known as the "Fearsome Fourth-some," the fourth-grade teaching quartet at Chesterfield Intermediate School.

Sheryl decides to break the silence by saying, "Hey, gang. How's it going with the Terrible Trio?" Her query was met with mutterings like "okay," "could be better," and "hangin' in there." Sheryl entered the lounge during this time of the day hoping to hear updates regarding a budding faculty romance, last week's high school football game, today's school board election, or yesterday's playground scuffle, but those expectations fell flat. She knows that these topics would have readily been discussed in the past, but since being named the building's assistant principal, Sheryl has been ostracized from most conversations with her former teaching partners as well as most of the Chesterfield faculty.

Sheryl feels like the teachers are blaming her for central office decisions made at the end of last school year. They reduced the number of fourth grade teachers from four to three, thus increasing the number of students in each fourth grade class. An assistant principal's position was created to help alleviate the workload of Principal Marcie McPhearson, who will retire in two to three years. Ms. Shannon feels like she was a previously valued faculty member, as her peers named her Teacher of the Year for two consecutive years. Now, unfortunately, Ms. Shannon is not so sure that they hold her in the same regard.

Discussion

1. Is it common for teachers to ostracize a former teacher who has been assigned administrative duties? Why or why not?
2. Who could Ms. Shannon consult with regarding her feelings at this time?
3. What actions could the following people take to help Ms. Shannon: (a) central office; (b) Ms. McPhearson; and, (c) the fourth grade teachers?

Cheating on the Test

Case

Emily Emerson, a teaching assistant at Midway High School, is proud of the students she tutored this school year to retake the state's required tests. For the past five years, she built an outstanding reputation in the district for helping struggling students pass these highstakes exams. Students who had repeatedly failed the tests were successful after being tutored by Ms. Emerson. The school's guidance counselor, Janice James, and testing coordinator, Holly Hobbs, always felt confident with placing the most at-risk students with Emily. Both Ms. James and Ms. Hobbs referred to her as their "miracle worker." Ms. Emerson confides with Janice and Holly that she knows these students will do as well as students in the past, even though this remaining group was infamous for performing poorly.

Ms. Hobbs traditionally assigned Ms. Emerson to be a test monitor because the students viewed her as their "good luck charm." Emily strolled around the room while the students took their exams, occasionally pausing to look at student responses to various test items. She was careful not to give any sort of indication that a student may have provided a wrong answer. As the students turn in their completed tests, Emily gives each student a "thumbs up" and one of her contagious smiles, indicating to them that she felt confident they passed. The students always mirrored the gestures as their way of saying, "Thanks, for your help."

After the last student submits their test booklet to Ms. Hobbs, the other test monitor, the cell phone in Ms. Hobbs' purse rings. The only statement Emily clearly heard was Ms. Hobbs saying, "I'll be right there." Holly briefly explained that there was an emergency involving her son at the elementary school. As she scurried out of the library, she said, "Emily, be a dear and take the test booklets to the counselor's office where Ms. James will seal each booklet before sending them off to be graded." "That won't be a problem, Holly," assures Emily.

Janice was not in her office when Emily brought the box of test booklets in to be processed. She was familiar with the processing steps, as Ms. James had her complete these mundane tasks in the past. Ms. Emerson knew what needed to be done. She sat at Ms. James' desk, pulled the first booklet out, and began her usual routine. After completing twelve of the twenty booklets, Emily is startled by Janice sharply asking, "Ms. Emerson, what are you doing with that eraser?"

Discussion

1. What should Ms. James do at this point?
2. What actions need to be taken with: (a) Ms. Emerson; (b) Ms. Hobbs; (c) Ms. James; and, (d) the twenty test takers?
3. Who is responsible for this breech in test security? Explain your answer.
4. What ethical questions arise from this scenario?

Collecting Funds for Social Concerns

Case

There seems to be an inordinate amount of collecting for social concerns recently at Hilltop High School. Funds are collected almost daily for various social concerns, such as birthdays, baby showers, retirements, condolences, etc. Several teachers have voiced their displeasure with the constant collections and indicated that they will have to stop their charity if the number of collections does not taper.

Discussion

1. Is this a problem for all schools that must be endured? Explain.
2. How can this problem be resolved?
3. Is it the responsibility of the administration to oversee this? Why or why not?
4. What if the Hilltop staff wants to chip in to buy lottery tickets or gamble?

Communicating Through Proper Channels

Case

Garrison Grandy, the curriculum director for the past five years at Jordan Woods School District, attends a May meeting at the regional educational service center. A prominent speaker addresses the crowded congregation of area school administrators about integrating curricular concepts as a means of increasing instructional time. During a scheduled break in the presentation, Dr. Grandy notices a fellow Jordan Woods administrator across the room. Garrison weaves his way through the clumps of visiting school officials toward Vic Vanderhausen, a principal at the district's alternative high school. En route, Garrison notes several surrounding attendees patting Vic on the back, shaking his hand, and sending various congratulatory messages his way. Dr. Grandy assumes that these gestures are offered for Mr. Vanderhausen's recent marriage, which was Garrison's purpose for making his trek across the packed venue.

Upon spotting Garrison halfway across the room, a "deer in the headlights" expression flashed onto Vic's face. Garrison thought this reaction was peculiar, but he brushed it off as a simple, off-the-cuff reflex for being so unduly receptive to the showering adulations. Dr. Grandy was about eight feet away from Mr. Vanderhausen when Dr. Grandy heard one of the service center's directors exclaim, "Hey, Victor! I heard the good news from Connie Sue Collins a couple of weeks ago. Congratulations on being named the new curriculum director at Jordan Woods!"

These last statements caused Garrison to stop in his tracks, as he was shocked to hear about any administrative changes at Jordan Woods. The only apparent change was that of Ms. Collins replacing the current retiring superintendent in July. To further add to Dr. Grandy's confusion, he confidentially asked Ms. Collins two days ago if there were any administrative changes forthcoming in her administrative team. Connie assured Garrison that things would remain status quo. Garrison quickly changed course, making his way out the meeting room's door so that he could confront Connie Sue Collins.

Discussion

1. What communication medium should Dr. Grandy use in confronting Ms. Collins? Explain your response.
2. Should Dr. Grandy confront Mr. Vanderhausen at this point? Later?
3. What could Dr. Grandy read into Ms. Collins' earlier statement to him versus what has allegedly occurred? Explain your thoughts.
4. What communication channel(s) should have been used so that such an awkward revelation could be avoided? Describe the different communication options.

Comparing Students' Efforts During a Parent-Teacher Conference

Case

Mike McMillan, the principal at Kemp Elementary School, drops in on a scheduled meeting between a second-grade teacher, Lucinda Lickhardt, and the parents of Scott Scarborough. Ms. Lickhardt notified Mr. McMillan via a school email earlier in the day about scheduling this conference, as this was a standard procedure when parents request an after-school meeting. Scott struggles with his writing, and the Scarboroughs want to meet with Ms. Lickhardt to see what they could do to help with their son's efforts. In her email, Lucinda indicates that she is not pleased with scheduling this impromptu appointment, but she has unselfishly rearranged her personal daily schedule many times during her twenty-eight year stint at Kemp and will do so again to accommodate the parents' work schedules.

Mr. McMillan enters the room shortly after the designated 3:45 start. Handshakes and brief introductions are made between the parents and principal. Ms. Lickhardt resumes the meeting by stating, "Mr. McMillan, the Scarboroughs are here to discuss their concerns about their son's efforts in writing. I told them that I've been worried about Scott's efforts in all subjects, but I needed to keep this meeting brief due to a prior commitment on my personal calendar and due to them needing to get to their shifts on time. So, let's get on with this." Mr. Scarborough scratches his head and says, "I don't know why Scott is struggling so much this year. He had a good first grade experience, and his grades indicated that. His first grade teacher told to us that Scott was a very bright and creative boy. So far this year, all his grade reports indicate that he is doing poorly. What skills does a second grader need to demonstrate?"

"Well since you only indicated you wanted to talk about his writing, I've got something to show you," says Ms. Lickhardt as she opens a desk drawer and reveals Scott's writing journal. Lucinda leafs through the spiral notebook and notes Scott's primitive penmanship and each entry's brevity. "He seldom produces more that a sentence or two, and that's after constant goading him to write more." Mrs. Scarborough is intrigued, and asks, "What prompts did you use for this entry, Ms. Lickhardt?" "I have a standard writing prompt. I ask them to write about what they did yesterday; however, I do vary the prompt if they are writing on a Monday. When it's a Monday I have them tell me about what they did over the weekend."

Lucinda reaches into the desk drawer and retrieves another writing journal. "You see this is the caliber of work submitted by another student. Note her neat cursive writing and the length of her entries," asserts the teacher. The Scarboroughs start comparing the two journals' entries. "As a matter of fact, I strongly suspect that this girl has a learning disability, but I don't think she will qualify for special education services. So, you see why I'm so concerned about Scott, too?" quips Ms. Lickhardt. Mr. McMillan squirms in his chair hoping that this conference concludes quickly.

Discussion

1. What are some concerns emerging from this conference?
2. How could Mr. McMillan approach Ms. Lickhardt with those concerns?
3. Should teachers receive training on how to conduct conferences? Why or why not?

Compiling a Substitute Teachers Handbook

Case

Winifred Wilson, the principal at Shelton Glen High School, informs Larry LeBlanc, the new assistant principal that he will be responsible for orienting substitute teachers to their building. "You may handle this matter in any way that you see fit," charges Ms. Wilson. Mr. LeBlanc witnessed his predecessor constantly informing substitutes about various school procedures and practices each time they reported for duty. Because Larry taught at SGHS for six years prior to being named assistant principal, he was familiar with the school's teachers' handbook. He thought a similar manual for substitute teachers could be the answer to effectively orienting substitute teachers.

Discussion

1. What should Mr. LeBlanc consider including in the substitute teachers' handbook?
2. Who could help Mr. LeBlanc compile the necessary information? Justify your choices.
3. What are common procedures used in schools for substitute teacher orientation?

Configuring Central Office Personnel Needs

Case

Dr. Kelton Kraus, superintendent of Graham City School District, anticipates the upcoming re-election campaign for the head of the teachers' union. The current leader, Herman Henderson, is practically guaranteed to win; however, a reliable source indicates that Mr. Henderson plans to embellish his campaign with criticisms directed at Dr. Kraus' administrative management. The source further explains that Mr. Henderson intends to convince union members that the district's central office is overloaded with administrative staff and that no teacher raises can be allocated because of those administrative salaries creating such a heavy financial drain.

Dr. Kraus has approximately three months to make some changes prior to the time the anticipated re-election campaign begins. He has privately wondered about the central office staff configuration he inherited two years ago. Recently, several supervisors complained that they were inundated with work and needed additional personnel to help. Dr. Kraus looks over the organizational chart and observes there are three administrative areas in the city, each having approximately three high schools, six middle schools, and twelve elementary schools. Each area office has the following staff: (a) an assistant superintendent for each area; (b) two secretaries for each assistant superintendent; (c) separate instructional supervisors for science, mathematics, social studies, music, language arts, foreign language, art, physical education, reading, shop, drivers education, testing, and special education.

Discussion

1. Draw an organizational chart graphically depicting the positions within the area offices.
2. Is there truly an overage of central office administrators? Explain your answer.

3. Why do the central office personnel think they need more help?
4. Is the union president right about the reason for the lack of funds for teacher raises? Why or why not?
5. What should Dr. Kraus do about the staffing issue? What should Dr. Kraus do about the union president?

Confronting an Influential Booster Group

Case

The Caldwell High School Band has steadily improved its quality and enrollment over the past several years. The Band Boosters, as a result, have become an influential support group as they help with finances, serve as chaperones, and assist as equipment movers at various performances.

Unfortunately, the well-supported band director, Brad Bryant, is accused of unethical conduct at district contests, and several band members affirm these charges' veracity. The district personnel director, Charles Chastain, assesses a suspension without pay reprimand to Mr. Bryant. This disciplinary action is disclosed only to the band director; however, several Band Booster parents learn about the penalty and request a meeting with Tom Tolliver, the district superintendent.

At the meeting, the Band Booster representatives confront Mr. Tolliver with charges that Mr. Bryant's penalty is unjust. Additionally, they demand dismissing the district's disciplinary measures. They further assert that if nothing is changed regarding this matter, they refuse to support any upcoming school levies and they will take the matter to next school board meeting.

Discussion

1. Mr. Tolliver listened to the Band Booster representatives in a closed meeting for approximately three hours. What is a viable response he could have to their request?
2. What could Mr. Tolliver tell them, and what could he not reveal to them concerning the dilemma?
3. With whom could Mr. Tolliver review the Band Boosters' concerns?

4. What information should Mr. Tolliver gathered before you meet with the booster representatives?
5. With this situation obviously going through the "rumor mill," what are the ramifications for the district? Explain your answer.
6. How should Mr. Tolliver respond to staff, parents, and/or community members who confront him about this issue?

Considering a Mandatory Drug Testing Program

Case

A recent survey of students at Noone Intermediate School (grades 4–6), Dusque Junior High School (grades 7–8) and Sunset High School (grades 9–12) indicated that many students on those campuses were experimenting with illegal drugs and alcohol. The survey's results were discussed at a recent school board meeting. The board charged Superintendent Sonny Moon to find an immediate solution to this problem.

The superintendent formed an ad hoc committee to investigate the feasibility of implementing a drug-testing program at those campuses. A consensus attained by the committee determined that drug testing every student attending school at Noone, Dusque, and Sunset was warranted.

The ad hoc committee members rationalized that students at those campuses are required by the state education department to take a series of criterion-referenced exams in various subject areas. Results from these mandated exams determine campus-level and district-level "report card" ratings, which in turn are reported by local and statewide media. Illegal substance abuse impairs the mental capabilities of students who engage in such activities. Impaired students adversely affect the campus and district ratings; therefore, the district has a compelling interest to drug test every student in the grades where the state exams are given.

Discussion

1. Did the ad hoc committee formulate a valid rationale for implementing a drug-testing program? Why or why not?
2. Describe some potential barriers the district may encounter if they follow the committee's recommendation.

3. What are some possible reactions from the following affected groups: (a) students, (b) parents, (c) teachers, (d) community members, and (e) the state education department?
4. If you were Sonny Moon would you forward this proposal to the school board? Why or why not?

Considering a New Budgeting Approach

Case

Trudy Tidwell, the principal at Lamar Elementary School, receives a budget review request from the district's budget director. Faculty and staff costs are fixed and are not within Ms. Tidwell's control. The areas needing review include: (a) equipment replacement; (b) new equipment; (c) books and supplies; (d) secretarial supplies; and, (e) janitorial supplies

Trudy remembers reading about zero-based budgeting in the finance class she took while getting her principal's license. She walks over to her office bookcase and pulls the textbook used in that course off of the shelf. Trudy thumbs to the section concerning zero-based budgeting and refreshes her memory about its recommended processes.

According to the text, she should ask all concerned personnel to review last year's budget. Following this, they should initiate a new plan and determine: (a) what they absolutely must have to run a minimum competency operation; then determine; (b) what they would want budgeted in order to do an adequate job with little or no frills; and, (c) what they would like to have if the district received a lot of money and all could have their "wish lists" fulfilled.

Discussion

1. How can Ms. Tidwell prioritize the five areas given to her by the district budget director? Should she list the areas in order of importance? Should she ask for anyone's help?
2. What are your thoughts about the concept of a zero-based budget?
3. How could Ms. Tidwell go about trying this new budgeting scheme?
4. How many people should Ms. Tidwell involve in her building's zero-based budgeting? Who would they be?

Controlling Library Censorship

Case

Several students at Fayetteville High School submitted a written complaint with Principal Ed Eagleton about what they perceive as unwarranted censorship of library materials. The students contend that classic books such as "Catcher in the Rye," "The Adventures of Huckleberry Finn," and "Catch 22" are not on the library shelves. Some books contain thick, black markings that mask words, and in other books, pages have been completely removed. Various issues of the magazine, "National Geographic," are unavailable for students' perusal. Teachers have also complained about various editorial cartoons being cut out of newspaper due to their unflattering caricatures of various political figures. They also claim that the librarian refuses to purchase the video, "Schindler's List," due to its graphic content.

The librarian, Marian Millet, is a thirty-year veteran of Fayetteville schools, and she has served as the FHS librarian for the past twenty years. Mr. Eagleton knows that Ms. Millet is quite a religious person, as she and her family regularly attend the same church as the Eagletons. In fact, Marian is Ethan Eagleton's Sunday school teacher. Mr. Eagleton schedules a meeting with Ms. Millet tomorrow concerning the allegations.

Discussion

1. How could Mr. Eagleton approach Ms. Millet with these complaints?
2. Does Ms. Millet have a right to withhold these items from circulation? Why or why not?
3. What are some viable ways of handling these students' concerns?

Controlling the Release of Students from School

Case

Melba Montgomery, the secretary at Franklin Elementary School, indicates to Paula Peterson, the principal, that there is a problem unfolding. Melba describes the recent events. A female parent wants to withdraw her son, Andre, from school. While the mother is in the outer office, Melba receives a telephone call from an adult male stating he is Andre's father and that under no circumstances should the child be allowed to leave school. Melba remembers the father enrolling Andre last month when they arrived from out of state. Andre's father states that the child's mother is mentally unstable, and he further explains that he is seriously considering divorce but has not filed any papers to that effect. "Ms. Peterson, what do I do now?" asks Ms. Montgomery.

Discussion

1. What should Paula Peterson do?
2. Who has custody of the child?
3. Should the child be allowed to go with the mother? The father? Why?
4. Can a policy be developed to help out in cases like this?

Controlling Violence in a Special Education Classroom

Case

Michael Mansford, a six-year old Autistic boy, is placed in his elementary school's support room for students with multiple-handicaps. A broad range of disabilities exists in this classroom, and behavioral issues are common. For example, Michael's outbursts tend to be violent and extremely aggressive. His Autism requires a strictly regimented schedule. Deviating from his schedule usually brings on one of his outbursts.

Past outbursts included actions such as running away, throwing objects, hitting, spitting, and screaming. Historically, Michael's physical aggressions involved only adult staff members. Today during an outburst, he threw a dictionary that shattered a window. Michael pushed some students as he attempted to escape out of the broken window. Some glass chards fell into a nearby student's hair; otherwise, no students were injured.

Discussion

1. If you were Michael's classroom teacher, what would you do about this situation? Who do you involve to help you make your decisions (i.e., parents, school psychologist, principal)?
2. Would suspending Michael be an appropriate action? Why or why not?
3. What kind of disciplinary consequences are appropriate for students with Autism?
4. To what extent have you considered the rights of Michael's classmates to learn in a safe environment, without the fear of injury? Explain.
5. Within a classroom environment such as the one described, who would be liable in the event of a serious injury?

Dealing With an Ineffective Principal

Case

The Vanderbilt Middle School faculty was grateful about having the opportunity to interview and select a new building principal. The superintendent, Dr. Judith Jennings, and the personnel director, Fred Fellows, respected the faculty's recommendation and employed the faculty choice for principal, Mr. Duane Dixon. During Mr. Dixon's first semester, problem after problem surfaced causing the faculty to begin questioning their principal selection. Student discipline was not enforced, teachers were not supported, and Mr. Dixon was frequently away from the building when needed. A group of teachers discussed this sensitive issue with Mr. Fellows, and he, in turn, approached Dr. Jennings with their concerns. By the end of the school year, the Vanderbilt faculty was completely disheartened with Mr. Dixon. They crafted a letter to the superintendent and the personnel director requesting another administrator lead the building even though Mr. Dixon was only finishing the first year of his two-year contract.

Discussion

1. As superintendent, what approach(es) could Dr. Jennings take in dealing with this situation?
2. Who could Dr. Jennings communicate with as she attempts to bring this problem to resolution?
3. What does Dr. Jennings tell the school board, if anything?

Defending Against Discrimination Accusations

Case

Dr. Bob Billingsly is the superintendent of Union Center Schools, a predominantly blue-collar community. Ethnic minority students represent less than one percent of the district's enrollment; however, today a new female student, Maria Morales, enrolls into one of the district's elementary schools, Cooper Elementary. Helena Hernandez, Maria's mother, contacts Dr. Billingsly's office concerning what she alleges to be unfair disciplinary actions against her daughter pertaining to an incident that happened during yesterday's recess. In her conversation, Ms. Hernandez indicates that several "white" students made fun of Maria and called her names with racial overtones.

Before Dr. Billingsly has a chance to contact Cooper Elementary's principal, a local newspaper reporter calls. Chad Childers from the Union Center Chronicle asks Dr. Billingsly why he didn't attend the news conference late this morning to address or defend the school district against Maria Morales' discrimination accusations. Mr. Childers further informed Dr. Billingsly that Ms. Hernandez complained to the media about the alleged discrimination through a representative of a nationally recognized equal rights organization that is representing the family.

Discussion

1. What is Dr. Billingsly's first task in dealing with this situation?
2. List (in priority order) the different people Dr. Billingsly should contact concerning this issue.
3. Discuss your reasoning for the priority contact list in Question 2.
4. What information should Dr. Billingsly disseminate to the news media addressing this dilemma?
5. How should Dr. Billingsly address the media?
6. What ramifications does this type of situation have on school district policy?

Determining Board Members' Political Agendas

Case

The recent school board election results in Glendale indicate that the community wants change. Three newly elected members' campaign platforms pledged to make dramatic changes to the current "inefficient and incompetent" school board. Landon Logan, Olivia O'Keefe, and Craig Cunningham vow to show their constituency that their actions back up their campaign promises. Superintendent Karen Kensington is concerned about the coalition's promises as these newly elected school board members outnumber the incumbents, three to two.

Discussion

1. What should Dr. Kensington do about this situation? Explain your answer.
2. Does this mean she and her assistants should resign? Why or why not?
3. Who can Dr. Kensington go to for help? Community members? Parents? Teachers? Students? How?

Determining Classified Personnel Job Descriptions

Case

"That's not my job," firmly stated the office clerk to her new principal, Alice Anniston. Alice assumed her duties at Freemont Elementary a few weeks ago and she was still struggling with remembering staff members' names; much less the particular tasks they were contracted to perform. The terse remark caused Alice to wonder what the clerk's specific job description contained, as well as the job descriptions of other classified employees. She searched the office files for classified employee job descriptions, but found none. Ms. Anniston called the central administration office and asked the personnel director about classified employee job descriptions. The personnel director indicated that there were a few job descriptions, but they were over fifteen years old. Alice is concerned about the potential morale problems that may arise from her lack of knowledge about past office practices as well as the lack of written job descriptions for classified employees.

Discussion

1. Are job descriptions really necessary? Explain your answer.
2. How should they be developed if they are to be used?
3. Who should be involved in the development of job descriptions?
4. Can you think of any reasons why job descriptions might not be a good idea?

Determining Homework Accountability

Case

Nancy Nelson, a parent of two students at Twin Lakes Middle School, informs Superintendent Charles Chesterfield that she objects to her children being assigned homework at school. Ms. Nelson claims that homework encroaches on her parental prerogative and the children should not be held accountable for work done at home.

Discussion

1. What should Mr. Chesterfield tell Ms. Nelson?
2. Does the case have any legal merit? Explain your answer.
3. Should homework assigned by the schools? Why or why not?
4. Should the district devise guidelines for assigning homework?
5. Who should make the guidelines?
6. Should school personnel punish students failing to do their homework? Explain your answer.

Determining Teacher Effectiveness

Case

At a recent meeting of the Clarkstown School District Board of Education, Matt Mendelson, a board member, proposes that annual teacher raises be based on merit. After considerable discussion, the board proposed a policy that they contend provides a "measurable basis" for assessing teacher merit. They desire the new rating scale to be implemented this school year. Their rating scale considers the following: (a) determine the teacher's standing in the community; (b) rate teaching rather than teachers; (c) rely on several judgments rather than one person's judgment; (d) utilize every available means and method towards determining teacher efficiency; (e) analyze the teacher's attendance and service records; and, (f) include feedback from parents and students.

Discussion

1. What method is normally used to evaluate teachers?
2. What method should be used? Why?
3. Can desirable teaching qualities be determined quantitatively? Why or why not?
4. Is a self-rating system viable? Why or why not?
5. Is "pupil progress" the best measurable outcome?
6. Is it reasonable to assume immediate implementation of such a plan?
7. Which of the items should be used? Explain your answers.
8. Which of the items should be deleted? Explain your answers.

Developing a Safety Program

Case

Pete Perkins, principal at Forest Glen Elementary School, wiped the tears from his eyes after reading the newspaper's account of Caitlyn Crawford's accident. Yesterday evening, this first-grader was struck and killed in the street outside her home. The faculty is visibly shaken by the tragedy. Several saddened faculty members stopped by the office to talk with Mr. Perkins about how this accident could have been prevented if safety issues were emphasized more in their school curriculum. Pete considers adopting a comprehensive public safety program as a response to this incident, but he wonders if this program will gain the community's support.

Discussion

1. Should Mr. Perkins feel obligated to include a public safety program to his school's curriculum? Is it a good idea? Or, should he insist that parents and guardians provide this type of training?
2. What would be the objectives of a comprehensive safety program?
3. Do you think the entire faculty would support this effort? Why or why not?
4. Describe how he could enlist the support of the community?
5. Who could Mr. Perkins get to teach the program?

Developing Classroom Management Expectations

Case

At a recent Hamilton Middle School faculty meeting, Principal Mick Marley, asked the veteran staff members to develop classroom management criteria. Mr. Marley compiled a "top ten" list that consisted of the following: (a) use seating charts, routines, procedures; (b) don't smile until Thanksgiving; (c) use written plans; (d) arrive early, stay late; (e) never accept excuses from students; (f) have work on the board when students arrive; (i) if the lesson isn't going well, stop and assign a study hall; (j) vary activities and teaching techniques; (k) keep students busy; and, (l) avoid arguing with students.

Discussion

1. Is it possible to have "rules" that will help new teachers? Why or why not?
2. Which of the above are good ideas, and why? Which are not, and why?
3. Can you think of anything to add to the list?

Developing Special Educational Job Descriptions

Case

Amy Armstrong and Mavis McPherson have worked as special education aides for over ten years in rooms for children with multiple disabilities. They are both very aware of the requirements listed on their job descriptions. Some of the job descriptions include: wiping noses, changing diapers, feeding students, and "other duties as assigned," as stated in their contract. A student who moved into the district halfway through the school year requires catheterization twice daily, as well as, an occasional suppository. Neither aide is willing to perform these essential tasks for the new student. Karen Kildare, the district's special education supervisor, needs to decide what to do about this situation.

Discussion

1. What recourse does Ms. Kildare have with these unwilling workers?
2. Describe the probable sequence of events that could occur in the conference that Ms. Kildare could conduct with these employees.
3. Both aides appear to be loyal employees, how could Ms. Kildare achieve a win-win situation between the needs of the organization and the willingness of these employees?

Disclosing Sensitive Issues

Case

A staffing committee for Bridgeport Schools, recently appointed by Superintendent Rochelle Runnells, consists of personnel from the central office, supervisors, building principals, assistant principals and selected parents from schools throughout the district. The principals were asked to comment on staffing needs for the upcoming school year and possible non-renewal of teaching contracts for poor performing teachers. The committee failed to progress very far and adjourned without making any decisions. Several days later, a principal who was at the meeting, Tom Turner, received a visit from three very indignant teachers demanding to know why their names were on a "to be fired" list. They threatened legal action, insisting their teaching performance was considered better than satisfactory, and indicated they had the support of many community members. Mr. Turner knew the confidential information they received was divulged from someone at the staffing committee meeting.

Discussion

1. What would you recommend the principal do now?
2. Will the unauthorized disclosure affect the termination process if the teachers are later considered incompetent?
3. How can problems like this be avoided? Are they inevitable?
4. What actions are required before a teaching contract is not renewed?
5. Is non-renewal the same thing as being fired?
6. Could the teachers sue and have a chance of regaining their jobs?

Dismissing an Administrator

Case

Dr. Rhonda Rambeck is in her first year as superintendent for the Woodmere School District. She finds one central office director, Marilyn Manchester, to be extremely lax in her work. Ms. Manchester comes and goes as she pleases, with questionable work hours. When Dr. Rambeck discusses her concerns with the Ms. Manchester, the director simply indicates her job is district-wide, and if she is not in her office, she is in a school or at a social agency helping the students in the district

Several school district teachers and administrators bring numerous complaints about Ms. Manchester to Dr. Rambeck's attention. The school board members hear about this, and bring the issue to the superintendent for resolution. To make the situation even more complex, Marilyn has worked for the district in several capacities over the last twenty-five years and has a teacher contingency supporting her. Dr. Rambeck feels these teachers will defend Ms. Manchester if she is confronted again with questions regarding her job performance.

Discussion

1. Given the background information of the case, what steps could Dr. Rambeck take in addressing this situation?
2. How can Dr. Rambeck assure district level administrators are ethical about their work and time given to the job?
3. Can Dr. Rambeck legally dismiss an administrator for questionable work hours?

Displaying Inappropriate Public Behavior

Case

Barbara Brazier has been the principal at Andrews Elementary School for the past nine years. She feels she is a substitute parent for many of her lower income students and frequently hugs them at school and whenever she sees them in public. The students appreciate her attention and affection.

The local high school basketball games are big community events, which Ms. Brazier often attends showing her support for her former students. Her favorite seat on a top row bleacher provides optimum view for monitoring the behavior of her current students. Barbara, a former university basketball standout, coached basketball prior to becoming a school administrator.

Recently at a girls' basketball game, the boys' team star center, spots Barbara in the crowd. "Yo, Ms. Brazier!" yells Jerome Jacoby from the gymnasium concourse. He waves and displays a wide toothy grin at his former school principal. Barbara barely recognizes this formidable 6'4" athlete as the troubled little boy she frequently counseled in her office. She waves and shouts back, "Come here you little scamp!"

Jerome leaps up the gym bleachers, politely clearing his path as he bounds toward Ms. Brazier. Without hesitation, he gives Barbara a big hug and a peck on the cheek. She automatically returns the affections. During their exchange, Jerome accidentally smears cotton candy in Barbara's hair and her lipstick smudges his cheek. Ms. Brazier asks Jerome about his current events. Being a good storyteller, tonight being no exception, Jerome's tales were peppered with much exaggeration frequently bringing outbursts of laughter from Barbara.

During a laughing episode, Jerome notices the cotton candy in Barbara's hair, and says, "Yo, Ms. Brazier, you've got some of my candy in your hair. Let me get it out." Jerome reaches over, gingerly pulling the sticky goo from Ms. Brazier's hair. Barbara, still reeling from his last escapade, exclaims, "You're a still a bad little boy, Jerome! I'm going to bend you over my knee and give you what I should have years ago." Ms. Brazier grabs Jerome's arm after he completes the cotton candy mission, and whimsically throws the boy over her lap. "You bad, bad boy!" shrieks Barbara comically as she swats Jerome's backside. They both laugh throughout the roughhousing. Jerome tops off the horseplay by plopping into Barbara's lap and giving her one last hug before scampering to join his teammates warm-up for their upcoming game.

Across the gym staunchly sits the school board president taking mental notes of an outrageous and inappropriate public display by a district employee.

Discussion

1. If you were the district superintendent, how would you handle the telephone call from the school board president about this incident?
2. If you were the district superintendent would you support Ms. Brazier? Why or why not?
3. Did Ms. Brazier and Jerome Jacoby display "outrageous and inappropriate" actions? Explain your answer.

Dueling Supervisory Authorities

Case

Linda Lawson, the principal at Western Hills Elementary School, makes random classroom visits a part of her supervisory duties. While conducting one of these visits, she noted that fourth grade teacher, Marsha Metcalf, was leading her class in a music lesson during the time normally devoted to mathematics instruction.

At an appropriate break during the lesson, Ms. Lawson privately queries Marsha about the impromptu curricular revision. Ms. Metcalf indicated that the district's music supervisor, James Jefferson, directed the building's teachers to "double up" their music instruction during the next three weeks as the fourth grade students prepare for a public musical performance.

When Ms. Lawson contacts Dr. Jefferson about this matter, he contends that the musical performance will be disastrous without the increased rehearsals. From Linda's tone on the phone, James senses the need to affirm that this temporary instructional revision squarely rests within his supervisory authority. Linda is miffed by the musical mandate and wonders what to do next.

Discussion

1. If you were Linda and James, what would you do next?
2. What long-term effects could result from this situation? Explain your answers.
3. If you were the district superintendent, would you intervene? Why or why not?
4. By diagram, illustrate appropriate relationships between superintendent, principal(s), supervisors, and teachers.

Eliminating Underclassman Hazing

Case

Since Garden City High School was founded in the early 1920s, the incoming freshmen are initiated into high school life by the next year's senior class. These rituals traditionally coincide with an annual community-wide spring festival held around the small town's courthouse square. At the time of the festival, the schools are no longer in session; therefore, a large number of people attend and participate in the downtown activities.

In separate male and female groupings, the fledglings perform various activities prescribed by the upper classmen. The "initiation" activities traditionally include wearing clothing wrong side out, pushing pennies with your nose down the sidewalk, selling squares of toilet paper, face painting, singing "praise" songs to the seniors-to-be, egg-tossing contests, water balloon tossing contests, etc. Participation in these initiation activities is optional; however, peer pressure dictates that participation is expected.

In recent years, the activities have gradually drifted away from the downtown area to more secluded rural sites. Rumor has it that the activities have become more degrading to the underclassmen now that the activities are no longer conducted in such a public fashion. Reports indicate that underclassmen are forced to: (a) wrestle peers in a pit filled with a concoction of mud and excrement; (b) participate in wet t-shirt and underwear contests; (c) consume bugs and other animal parts; and, (d) endure being yelled at if they opt to not participate in these activities.

An irate mother of an incoming freshman girl wrote a letter to the editor of the Garden City Gazette. In the signed letter, the mother complained about the abuses that her daughter recently suffered from the most recent springtime initiation. The freshman coed reportedly suffered verbal, mental, and physical abuse. Her mother questioned why the school condoned such harmful and humiliating activities. Furthermore, she fears that future initiations may escalate in their severity and ultimately lead to serious injuries or even death.

Discussion

1. Should the high school principal get involved in doing something about these traditional rites of spring? Why or why not?
2. What are some possible reactions from different segments of the community if changes are/are not made (alumni, parents, students, business leaders, festival organizers, etc.)? Explain your answers.

Enacting a Weapons Zero-Tolerance Policy

Case

Barbara Bilbrey notes an increase in teen violence within Delaney High School and its outlying community in the five years since beginning her term as principal. She was hopeful when the local school board implemented a zero-tolerance policy this school year. This policy forbids weapons on school grounds and requires mandatory dismissal from school for violators. Ms. Bilbrey just telephoned the superintendent notifying him about actions at DHS yesterday and today that prompted her to enact the new zero-tolerance policy.

Yesterday, two high school males, Lendall Lockhart and Justin Jacobs altercated and while it appeared they resolved their differences, it later became evident to Barbara that both boys still had bad feelings about each other. As they were leaving school, several students overhead Lendall yelling from his car at Justin that he would get him "one way or another." This last scene was reported to Ms. Bilbrey by a faculty parking lot monitor and the similar supporting student accounts trickled into the office concerning this same incident.

Today, Barbara makes a typical walk-through of the parking lot and discovers a weapon on the seat of Justin's car. Reasoning that the gun was in plain view, Ms. Bilbrey reaches into the car through drivers-side open window, picks up the gun, and calls the police to come get it. The police arrive and determine that the gun was a "BB" gun. Barbara rationalizes that a "BB" gun is a weapon, and that was when she initiated procedures to dismiss Justin Jacobs from school.

Discussion

1. Justin's father argues that the "BB" gun is just a toy. How would you rule?
2. Should Justin be dismissed from school? How long?

3. Should the police have been called? If yes, at what point should the police have been called? If no, explain why not.
4. Are metal detectors the answer? Explain your answer.
5. Can cars be searched? What about items in plain view?

Evaluating School Supply Procedures

Case

The school supply system at W.O. Wright Elementary School is called a "closed supply system" by its teachers. They are hoping that the new building principal, Chris Cowlings, will retain this system of distributing classroom supplies. Under this system, a locked room houses all the supplies. Only one teacher, Don Dunn, has a key for this room. Teachers needing supplies submit an "order" to Mr. Dunn, usually early in the morning. During the day, Don assigns his classes seatwork so that he can "fill" the day's supply orders. Occasionally, he has students accompany him to help in delivering the needed supplies to the various classrooms. When Mr. Dunn notices particular items running low, he informs the school secretary and she re-orders the desired items.

Discussion

1. What do you think about the supply system?
2. If you were Chris Cowlings, would you continue this supply system? Why or why not?
3. What alternatives does Chris have?
4. Who is responsible for Mr. Dunn's unattended classes when he is filling orders?
5. How accountable is this system?
6. How do other schools handle school supply needs?

Evaluating Support Staff Performance

Case

Fern Fenton, the principal at Falling Water Middle School, realizes that some support staff in her building are not performing an adequate job with their assigned classroom duties. One teacher, David DiSalvo, complains about his aide frequently leaving his room, and on several occasions David heard about her visiting with fellow teaching assistants in the staff lounge during the time designated for her to assist students in the classroom.

Another teacher, Tricia Turner, reports that her assistant befriends students who are her daughter's age and gossips about other students as she helps these "friends" with classroom assignments. Charley Chenowith, the 6th grade science teacher, complains about his aide refusing to clean the lab because that was not in her job description. Ms. Fenton further notices that several teaching assistants report to work clad in t-shirts and jeans. She is not pleased with the performances of these auxiliary staff members; however there is not an official evaluation instrument from which to assess these campus employees.

Discussion

1. What steps could Ms. Fenton take to eliminate these problems with the school's support staff?
2. Could Ms. Fenton fire these auxiliary staff based on the information she has at this point? Why or why not?
3. What would an evaluation instrument for teacher assistants look like? Describe its criteria and underlying descriptors.

Evaluating Teaching Effectiveness through Classroom Observations

Case

Sherry Stewart, the new principal at Piney Woods Elementary School, realizes that the faculty is not accustomed to having an administrator observe them teaching; furthermore, she feels unwelcome when she stops in many classrooms. For example, one veteran teacher, Paula Porter, was noticeably disturbed when Ms. Stewart walked in. Sherry was surprised when Ms. Porter pointedly asked whether she should expect frequent visits like this in the future.

On another occasion, Martin Minnix, promptly discontinued his teaching activity and gave his class a writing assignment. He casually strolled over to Ms. Stewart and asked her if there was anything wrong. Ms. Steward indicated that there wasn't anything wrong, and suggested that he resume the teaching activity he was conducting at the time she entered the room. Martin complied, but he was visibly annoyed. Sherry knew that her predecessor had the reputation of being office-bound and devoted little time to supervision, but didn't realize that it was such a problem.

Discussion

1. Are there supervisory techniques other than classroom visitation for the improvement of instruction? Discuss these approaches.
2. Is there any justification for the negative attitude of the staff toward Ms. Stewart's visits? Why?
3. Would it be better for her to give advance notice of her intended visit(s)? Why or why not?
4. Should Sherry Stewart discontinue the classroom visits? Why or why not?
5. If Ms. Stewart decides to continue the classroom visits, how can she do so in such a way as to arouse the least antagonism?

Extending Special Favors to School Board Members

Case

Transportation Director Sue Staniforth schedules a meeting with Superintendent Mark Martin. During their meeting, Sue informs Mark that a school board member, Joe Jeffries, called her three weeks ago and demanded that she have the school bus pick up his children at their residence. Mr. Martin looks up Jeffries' address in the phone book and realizes that the school board member's home is located in a neighborhood with many cul-de-sacs. The current transportation policy states that children living on cul-de-sacs must walk to designated waiting areas where they will be picked up and transported from those points. Sue instructed the route driver to pick up the Jeffries children at the location desired by their father. Ms. Staniforth further elaborates that since allowing this variance to the transportation policy, her office has been flooded with other residents wanting their children picked up at their front doors, too.

Discussion

1. What should be the first action Superintendent Martin takes in addressing this situation?
2. List several alternatives to dealing with this scenario.
3. Who could Mr. Martin consult concerning a solution to the problem, or is a solution really needed?
4. Are there legal ramifications to this issue? If so, what are they?
5. Is Mr. Martin responsible for bringing this issue to closure, or is the school board member? Why?

Grooming Standards for Student Teachers

Case

Scott Scoggins, a pre-service teacher from Western State University, is excited about his upcoming student teaching experiences at Fairview High School. As an art education major, he spent three years majoring in art and this past year he enrolled in several field-based education courses that whetted his passion for classroom teaching. Today, Scott is meeting with the FHS principal, Mark Madison, about his assignment. Scott realizes that in order to make a good impression he must depart from his collegiate uniform (t-shirt, shorts, and sandals) and he dons a new shirt, tie, pants, and shoes.

The two men exchange handshakes and introductions as Scott enters Mr. Madison's office. Mr. Madison directs Scott to sit in the chair across from his desk. Mark clears his throat and says, "Scott, I've reviewed your credentials, including several positive reference letters concerning your character and potential teaching abilities. I'm impressed, and I look forward to your semester here at Fairview High School. However, there are two things you need to do before entering one of our school's classrooms." Scott was pleased to hear the initial positive comments from Mr. Madison, but was concerned with his last statement.

"What two things do I need to do?" questions Scott. "Your nose ring and goatee must go. Our school dress code prohibits 'unusual' jewelry and male facial hair," curtly replies Mr. Madison. "I'm sorry, Mr. Madison, but I didn't know about these policies. WSU has no student dress code, and nothing was mentioned about the jewelry and facial hair when I observed classes at Crystal Falls High last term," explains Scott. "Well, Fairview is a much more conservative community than Crystal Falls. Mr. Scoggins, you're on our turf now," replies Mr. Madison. As he rises from his chair and motions to the door, Mr. Madison says, "We will continue our conversation when you return from completing the two tasks. Good day, Mr. Scoggins, and welcome to Fairview High."

Discussion

1. Did Mr. Madison handle this situation well? Why or why not?
2. What should Mr. Scoggins know before this meeting?
3. What could Mr. Scoggins do at this point?
4. What could the university do to help their pre-service teachers avoid this type of scene?

Grouping Grade Levels within a School District

Case

Ken Krenzel's first assignment as the Jackson County Schools' new supervisor of instruction is to prepare a plan for reorganizing the grade levels within the school district. Currently, this large suburban district has one high school (grades 10–12), three junior high schools (grades 7–9), and five elementary schools (grades K–6). A declining student population, reduced state and federal funds, aging facilities, and low standardized test scores promote the need for restructuring grade level assignments.

The district superintendent, Wendell Williams, proposes eliminating the junior high schools. He suggests that the elementary schools house grades K–8 while the high school serves grades 9–12. Assistant Superintendents Roxanne Rusk and Randy Roberts advocate organizing the schools in elementary schools (grades K–4), middle schools (grades 5–8), and a high school (9–12). A concerned parents group does not like the current grade groupings, and they are very concerned about Dr. Williams' plan for grades K–8 to be in housed within various district sites. This group desires only one to two grade levels being assigned to a building (i.e., grades K–1, grades 2–3, grades 4–5, grades 6–7, grades 8–9), and thus, keeping the current high school configuration (grades 10–12).

Mr. Krenzel assesses merit to each proposed plan. He favors limiting enrollment to one grade level per building except at the high school where he advocates housing grades 9–12. With several viable models to choose from, Ken concludes that he needs to appoint a committee to derive a proposal for the grade-level restructuring plan.

Discussion

1. Who should be appointed to serve on this committee? Explain your rationale for selecting each person.
2. Is it feasible to have a variety of grade-level configurations throughout the district?
3. Is one grouping method preferable to another? Why?

Guarding Against Possible HIV Contamination

Case

Debby Dotson, at teacher at Oaklawn High School, approaches Principal Mark McCleland with a problem. Debby's daughter, Denise, is an athletic trainer for the football team. As a trainer, one of Denise's duties includes taping players. Due to performing this task, she is in daily contact with all types of injuries, although none of the injuries are serious, many injuries do involve cuts and scrapes, thus potential exposure to blood. Recently, Denise overheard one player reveal to another player that he tested HIV positive, but intended to continue playing for the team. Denise informed her mother about what she overheard, and naturally, Ms. Dotson is very concerned about her daughter's safety. Debby requests that Mr. McCleland dismiss the HIV positive student. She further contends that if he does not act immediately, she will personally notify the OHS faculty, students, and parents of the potential danger lurking in their halls.

Discussion

1. What should Mark McCleland do?
2. What are the rights of the alleged HIV positive student?
3. What kind of school and community reaction can the Mr. McCleland expect when the word of this situation gets out?
4. Who should be notified that this has occurred? The superintendent? Public health officials? The parents? The community?

Handling a Crisis Situation

Case

Grover High School's principal, Josh Jennings, receives a phone call at 12:30 P.M. notifying him that a bomb will detonate in the building at exactly 2:00 P.M. Mr. Jennings immediately contacts Grace Guthrie, the district superintendent. Dr. Guthrie, in turn, arranges to meet Police Chief Mike Morrison at the threatened high school campus. When Grace arrives at GHS, it is obvious that the students and staff are aware of the situation as a few are standing outside looking at the spectacle as events unfold. Parents are arriving in droves to pick up their children, and are beginning to clog the parking lot entrances. As Dr. Guthrie nears the office, she sees several parents in the office, including a faculty member parent, arguing with Mr. Jennings over refusing to allow them to remove their children who are still inside the building. At the moment Dr. Guthrie begins to talk with Mr. Jennings, the police chief and several bomb detonation specialists arrive. Everyone appears to be waiting on Dr. Guthrie's decision on how to handle this growing crisis.

Discussion

1. Create a plan for Dr. Guthrie to address this emergency situation. Consider the following within the plan: (a) student, faculty, and staff safety; (b) school building inspection; (c) communication with parents and media; (d) responsibilities of high school administration; (e) school board awareness; and, (f) police and fire personnel responsibilities.
2. What approach should Dr. Guthrie take to address the concerns of the parents demanding their children leave the building immediately?
3. How should school personnel handle future bomb threat situations?
4. The absolute, final responsibility for student and staff safety during a potentially dangerous situation belongs to the: (a) superintendent; (b) school board; (c) high school administrators; (d) parents; (e) teachers; or (f) police and fire personnel? Defend your choice.

Handling a Disruptive Student

Case

In the upper right-hand corner of Jim Johnson's desk calendar is a small, penciled number, "125." Those are the number of days remaining until he retires from Stoneridge Elementary School. During his twenty-two year tenure as the building principal he prides himself on running a "tight ship." He has never expelled a child, but he fears that his first expulsion looms on the horizon. Within the first nine weeks of school, one female student has been referred to his office on numerous occasions from various classrooms. She has visited with Mr. Johnson for the following offenses: (a) turning desks over and disturbing other students; (b) kicking and hitting other students; (c) refusing to go with her class to the library and subsequently throwing herself to the floor kicking and screaming; (d) using profanity; and, (e) kicking a teacher and biting a teacher aide. Jim knows that he must make a decision soon regarding this student.

Discussion

1. What options are available to Jim Johnson?
2. How could the Jim's record on discipline effect the decision?
3. What special service organizations are available?
4. What rights do children have in school?
5. What rights do teachers have in school?

Handling a Split PTO

Case

Anne Alford is the recently appointed principal at Nicholas Elementary School, and as she assumes her new duties in July she meets with the former principal, Van Vernon. Anne expects Van to give her an overview of the building and faculty, but she is taken aback by his last revelation. Mr. Vernon warns Ms. Alford about the dissention among the school's Parent-Teacher Organization (PTO) membership.

Mr. Vernon explains that at the end of the school year, the PTO president and vice president had a major confrontation. Half the parents sided with the president, and half sided with the vice president. The disagreement concerning the focus and goals of the PTO was severe enough to divide the organization. Each group decides they are the official parent support group for the school, and refuses to relinquish control to the other.

With this knowledge, Ms. Alford schedules a meeting with the president and vice president in hopes of resolving the conflict. After three hours of discussion and disagreement, both PTO officers refuse to cooperate and work together. Moreover, they both demand to Ms. Alford that they be given full rights of heading the Nicholas Elementary School PTO.

Discussion

1. Ms. Alfred has listened carefully to both parties and their concerns. If you were Anne, what do you do at this point?
2. The initial relationship that Ms. Alford establishes with the parents is crucial to her gaining respect and support as the new building principal. Will her actions taken in Question 1 damage her ability to work with the parents? Why or why not?

3. What provisions could Anne Alford establish to lessen the chances of this type of situation happening in the future?
4. Is this a policy issue? Why or why not?
5. Should central office administrators be made aware of this problem? Why or why not?

Handling Common Transportation Problems

Case

Transportation Director Ken Killian receives written reports from the district's bus drivers. Mr. Killian forwards copies to the building principals prior to sending the drivers' reports to the superintendent's office. Martindale Middle School principal, Stan Sommers, had not heard anything recently about any bus problems; therefore, he assumed everything was going well in the student transportation area. The most recent reports he receives from Mr. Killian indicate otherwise. For example, student behavior is almost out of control on some routes. Items are thrown from buses and fights are almost a daily occurrence. Another report indicates that a parent boarded the bus on one route to discipline children who he claims were abusive to his daughters. The result was a shouting match between the man and several students including cursing and threatening language. This occurred at a stop that held up traffic until the driver persuaded the parent to leave the bus. Some other reported incidents include: (a) the drivers receive numerous requests for unauthorized stops and daily requests from students to allow friends to be dropped off with them; (b) one disruptive student refuses to identify himself to the driver and warns fellow students not to identify him at the risk of violence; and, (c) teachers release many students from class so late that the students miss their buses forcing them to walk or hitchhike home.

Discussion

1. What should Mr. Sommers do about these reports?
2. Should Mr. Sommers try to alleviate the situation before the superintendent's office receives the report? Why or why not?
3. Is it within Mr. Sommers' power to solve the dilemma? Explain.

Handling Complaints about Maintenance Personnel

Case

A recent principal's meeting at the Austin Heights School District was abuzz over maintenance service complaints. Most of these complaints centered on the following: (a) two maintenance personnel being dispatched to schools to do the work that one person could handle; (b) most maintenance personnel spend an inordinate amount of time drinking coffee and gossiping; (c) work orders are handled improperly with the longstanding policy of "first in, first out' not being uniformly followed; (d) unsafe conditions still exist at various district facilities, even after submitting several work orders for the same concern; (e) repairs appear slipshod and it is suspected that many times repairs are not actually made; and, (f) phone calls to the district office have resulted in little else than hollow promises.

Superintendent Doug Donaldson was surprised as he was unaware of these problems. His dealings with the district's maintenance supervisor, Ralph Riddell, were quite positive. Mr. Donaldson recalled the maintenance supervisor seemed like a very concerned and energetic person.

Discussion

1. What should Mr. Donaldson's actions be at this point?
2. What should Mr. Donaldson tell the principals?
3. What part of the problem is most disturbing to you? Explain your answer.

Handling Student Discipline Problems

Case

Sheldon Schumberg, the new principal at Rocky Ridge Elementary School, is concerned about enforcing discipline at his new assignment. His predecessor did little about the numerous fights she often considered as just "boys being boys." Mr. Schumberg notes numerous students roaming the halls at almost any time during the day. He thinks to himself, "Obviously, the teachers consider tardy students inevitable," as he personally observes them lingering in the halls following the bell that signals the onset of each new class.

During a recent faculty meeting, a veteran teacher asks Mr. Schumberg what is he going to do about student discipline at the Rocky Ridge Zoo? Another teacher pipes in that she thinks that today's children are completely unmanageable. These remarks receive a mixture of uncomfortable laughs with a spattering of applause. These remarks completely caught Sheldon off guard. He indicated that he would specifically address student discipline at their next meeting, and he quickly adjourned the current meeting.

Sheldon is not impressed with what he perceives to be low teacher morale, but his observations signal there are indeed pockets of excellence within Rocky Ridge. He can't quite determine why some teachers are successful and others are not. Mr. Schumberg's dealings with parents indicate that there is little consistency with discipline matters among the faculty. On some days students are suspended for offenses that on other days are handled in less punitive ways. The parents are very confused by these contradicting patterns of practice.

Discussion

1. From your perspective, this case study highlights what issue(s)?
2. Who should be involved in deciding what action(s) to take? Explain your answer.

3. Who is to blame for the discipline concerns at Rocky Ridge? Why?
4. Who should help develop disciplinary rules at this school? Why? List some school-wide rules that might help this situation.
5. How long will it take to see a change in the school?
6. What kind of problems will the Rocky Ridge personnel run into implementing this change?

Handling the Unauthorized Use of School Facilities

Case

Derek Dunningham, the assistant principal at Jackson Junior High School, drives past the school on his routine weekend scan. He can't help but notice a 45-foot commercial trailer parked in the teachers' reserved parking lot. The unhooked trailer occupies at least twelve spaces. In this urban setting, every parking space is utilized. Mr. Dunningham realizes that if the trailer is still there on Monday morning, there will be serious parking problems, snarled traffic patterns, and a host of irate parents and teachers.

Discussion

1. What can be done about this potential disaster before Monday morning?
2. Would pictures taken of the trailer today be helpful at a later date? Why or why not?
3. Should Derek take action or wait for instructions from the principal?
4. Should parking be permitted on school property when school is not in session? Explain your answer.
5. Who is responsible if the trailer damages the parking lot?
6. What can be done to avert such a situation in the future?

Harassing a Teacher: The Principal's Perspective

Case

Craig Cramer, the long-time principal at Flower Acres Elementary School, walks into Superintendent James Johnston's office. Craig received a message from James notifying him that an urgent meeting between the two was needed. Dr. Johnston starts the meeting by saying, "Craig, I need to talk to you about an issue involving Suzanne Schwartz. According to her, you are harassing her." Mr. Cramer looks confused and asks, "On what grounds, James?" Dr. Johnston reviews with Craig the notes taken during his and Ms. Schwartz's earlier meeting. Craig listens to Suzanne's interpretations of his classroom visits as relayed by James.

Mr. Cramer covers his face with his hands while shaking his head from side to side. Slowly lowering his hands, Craig explains, "Oh, my goodness, James. Suzanne is completely misinterpreting my reasons for stopping by her room so frequently. I started out simply checking to see if things were going all right for her as a new teacher and with her status as a new faculty member in our building. As the year progressed, I was getting parent phone calls about various problems in her classes. I didn't want to make her paranoid about her teaching abilities, so I never mentioned the specific reasons why I wanted to know how things were going. I thought that perhaps there were troubling situations in her personal life that could be affecting her classroom performance, so I did inquire about her personal life. Little did I know that she thought I was trying to 'hit' on her."

Dr. Johnston jots down notes while Mr. Cramer tells his rationale behind the classroom visits. Without any prompt from Dr. Johnston, Craig slaps his hand to his forehead and exclaims, "Now it makes sense!" "What are you talking about, Craig?" queries James. "Her reaction yesterday in the storage room. That's why she left in such a huff," replies Craig. He continues, "I was in the bookroom yesterday inventorying textbooks when Ms. Schwartz came in. She climbed that old rickety ladder to get some books on one of the upper shelves. I don't think she realized that the ladder was beginning to lean, so I quickly ran over and attempted to keep her from falling. Yes, I did touch her bottom, but it was for the purpose of preventing her from breaking something else." Dr. Johnston finishes writing down Mr. Cramer's side of the story.

Discussion

1. Did Mr. Cramer harass Ms. Schwartz? Explain your answer.
2. What could Mr. Cramer do to substantiate his claims?
3. Where did Mr. Cramer err in his supervisory capacities with Ms. Schwartz?
4. What could Dr. Johnston do at this point?

Harassing a Teacher: The Teacher's Perspective

Case

A meeting finished with an elementary teacher, Suzanne Schwartz, disturbs James Johnston, the superintendent of Shady Oaks Schools. In this meeting, Ms. Schwartz, a second-year teacher, accuses Craig Cramer, a long-time principal at Flower Acres Elementary School, of inappropriately making sexual advances towards her for the past two years. Obviously, Ms. Schwartz was quite shaken while revealing these charges to the superintendent, but she felt that something needed to be done.

James reviews the notes he scribbled while Ms. Schwartz recounted the events she feels constitute harassment. Suzanne revealed that Craig often dropped in her classroom after hours. Initially, she did not think anything about these visits as she felt that he was simply mentoring her through her early experiences at Flower Acres. The visits' frequency increased over time to the point where Mr. Cramer met with her daily. "He kept asking about how things were going inside and outside my classroom. I usually told him that things were 'okay,' and I felt that events going on outside of school time were my business. I never elaborated on any of that," related Suzanne.

The incident provoking her to come forward to Dr. Johnston happened yesterday. While Suzanne was on the textbook storage room's ladder, she felt a hand on her buttocks. The initial touch startled Suzanne because she had not heard anyone enter the room. She let out a small shriek, and quickly glanced around to see who was there. The hand belonged to Craig Cramer, who said, "I'm here for you." Suzanne told Dr. Johnston that she was so rattled by the inappropriate touch that she promptly left the storage room so as not to be alone with Mr. Cramer in the isolated area.

Discussion

1. Did Ms. Schwartz do the right thing in contacting Dr. Johnston? Explain your answer.
2. Is Ms. Schwartz overreacting to these situations? Why or why not?
3. What could help Ms. Schwartz substantiate her claims?
4. What action should Dr. Johnston take at this point?

Having Good Intentions but Setting a Bad Example

Case

An irate mother contacts the superintendent of Hale City Schools, Kevin Kenner, about her third grade son's recent conference with his principal. The child, Tommy Tuftman, is a chronic troublemaker at Duncan Elementary School, and his mother acknowledges that she is at wits end regarding his bad behavior at both home and school. Ms. Tuftman further explains to Mr. Kenner that it is difficult to try to teach Tommy acceptable social behaviors when he has a poor example in his school principal, Wendy Weirsom. Mr. Kenner asks Ms. Tuftman to explain herself.

"The other day, I was telling Tommy that he should not smoke cigarettes," explains Ms. Tuftman, "and he promptly snaps back that if cigarettes are so bad, why does Ms. Weirsom smoke them all the time? So, I asked him when did he see her smoking? He said she smoked all during the last meeting she had with him about his bad behavior at school." The last statement piqued Mr. Kenner's interest, as he had implemented a no smoking policy in all district buildings last year. He asked, "Was the conference between Tommy and Ms. Weirsom in her office?"

"No," replied Ms. Tuftman, "according to Tommy they were driving around town in her Cadillac. I can't believe the double standard this principal is setting for my child. Getting on to my son about his irresponsible behaviors, while puffing on a cigarette. Furthermore, Mr. Kenner, I did not know that a school employee could take my child off of school premises without my permission." Upon hearing this, Mr. Kenner feels compelled to do some investigating.

Discussion

1. Mr. Kenner should start his investigation with which individual?
2. Should Ms. Weirsom be reprimanded? Explain your answer.
3. If Mr. Kenner finds these allegations to be true, what steps should he take?
4. Was Ms. Weirsom's approach with Tommy appropriate? Explain your answer.

Hiring a New Building Principal

Case

A new principal will replace retiring principal, Adam Anderson, next year. Lincoln Elementary School teachers and parents have volunteered to be involved in the interview process that will name his successor. It was determined by the central office at Washington Heights School District that a team of six teachers and three parents would interview three finalists. The three finalists will be selected after the superintendent and personnel director screen the initial candidate applications.

Discussion

1. Should the Lincoln teachers or the Washington Heights superintendent make the final decision on hiring the new principal? Explain your answer.
2. In general, how should a school district formulate a procedure for hiring building principals?
3. Who should be involved in creating the hiring procedure?

Honoring a School Board Directive

Case

Don Douglas has served Western Hills School District as a building principal for the past seven years. He gained the respect of administrators, teachers, and the school board by improving student learning opportunities at Hilltop Middle School. At the March school board meeting, the board terminated Western Hills' superintendent due to insubordination. Following this decision, the board president immediately contacted Mr. Douglas informing him that he was appointed acting superintendent.

During his first meeting with the school board, Mr. Douglas was directed to initiate a plan for reorganizing all of the district's schools. The board insisted that these changes to the building grade levels would take effect this upcoming August when school resumed after the summer break. Don is concerned about the relatively short timeline remaining for such a complex task involving five elementary schools, a middle school, and a high school. The more Mr. Douglas delves into this directive, the more he thinks that there is insufficient time for making smooth transitions.

Discussion

1. What approach should Mr. Douglas take to express his concerns to the board of education?
2. Given the complexity of a comprehensive overhaul of Western Hills School District, list the priorities Mr. Douglas should take in initiating the task.
3. Who should be involved in this endeavor?
4. To what extent should the board of education be involved? Explain your answer.
5. What are the ramifications of a major overhaul district reorganization plan, even if the timeline for completion is reasonable?
6. Ideally, given the limited information you have concerning this district, what is a reasonable timeline for the reorganization?

Impeding the School's Custodial Services

Case

Gloria Gaston, the head custodian at Mt. Yukon Elementary School, reports to Principal Janice Jameson that she is experiencing the following difficulties. Ms. Gaston contends that these are some of the problems preventing her and other the custodial staff from accomplishing more work: (a) the younger students urinate on the bathroom floors causing a considerable mess; (b) paper towels are thrown all around the restrooms; (c) soap and whole toilet paper rolls are flushed in the toilets, creating back ups; (d) students verbally abuse her and the other custodial staff when the staff attempts to make on-the-spot behavior corrections; and, (e) teachers continually stop the custodians and ask them to do maintenance and fix-it orders.

Discussion

1. How can Ms. Jameson aid the custodial staff?
2. Describe a custodian's job description.
3. How should work orders be handled?
4. What kind of "chain of command" exists between the principal and the custodians? Are changes needed in this area? Why or why not?

Implementing a New Leadership Style

Case

Cole Crosby, the new superintendent at Hooverville School District, plans a retreat with the district's administrative staff. Mr. Crosby is quite aware of the former superintendent's autocratic leadership style, as it was well-known fact throughout this region of the state. Cole has not heard any negative comments from any of the district's administrative team about his predecessor's leadership style and is curious about how receptive they will be to his more collaborative approach.

Discussion

1. Discuss how Mr. Crosby could address the administrative team at the retreat.
2. With such an obvious contrast in leadership style, how can Mr. Crosby gain respect and support from the district administrators? Explain your answer.
3. Are there other qualities a new superintendent could have that would overshadow, in a positive way, the difference in leadership style?
4. Based on the situation, should Mr. Crosby try to change his leadership style to fit what the administrative team was accustomed to? Why or why not?

Improving Campus Staff Teamwork

Case

At a recent faculty meeting, Principal Harlan Hertzer, asked teachers to assist the campus custodial staff by doing the following: (a) collect trash in their classroom and place a can outside the classroom door for pickup; (b) assign students to place chairs on tops of tables and desks at the end of the day; (c) erase all writing surfaces (chalk or dry erase), collect chalk and/or markers and place them in their appropriate tray(s); (d) assign students to pick up litter and paper scraps off of the floor at the end of the day; and, (e) straighten rows of desks and tables.

The head custodian, Janice Jones, remarks to Mr. Hertzer that most teachers are following the requested actions, but one teacher, Bob Bullock, still leaves his classroom in a mess. Litter abounds, chairs are in disarray, writing surfaces are dirty, and trashcans scattered about the room are overflowing. When Ms. Jones asked Mr. Bullock why he didn't follow the principal's new recommendations, Mr. Bullock informed Ms. Jones that his teaching license and district contract didn't say anything about doing the janitor's job. Mr. Hertzer feels compelled to schedule an appointment with Mr. Bullock.

Discussion

1. If you were Mr. Hertzer, what would you say to Mr. Bullock? Ms. Jones?
2. Is the clean up list asking teachers to do something they were not hired to do? Explain your answer.
3. Review the above list. Which items would you object to? Would you add any items to the list?

Improving Custodial Services

Case

Yukon Elementary School, a twenty-year old building, is where Trina Truman is principal, and on each school day approximately five hundred students and forty adult staff use this facility. The custodian, Melvin Massey, inherited the land on which the school was built and in exchange for donating this parcel to the school district, he was granted lifetime employment as custodian. Recently, several concerns about the quality of custodial services have been brought to your attention. After several weeks of observation and casual inquiry, the following facts emerge about the duties the custodian performs alone. He: (a) unlocks all building doors promptly each morning an hour and a half prior to the beginning of school; (b) assists teachers in unloading supplies and other materials from their cars; (c) cleans all hallways and the cafeteria of debris each morning; (d) purchases needed supplies from various stores in town and directly hands the bills to the school secretary; (e) attempts to remove iron rust stains from the badly discolored toilet bowls and lavatories; (f) inspects toilet stalls daily and immediately scrubs off graffiti; (g) empties hallway trashcans once or twice per week; (h) wipes out drinking fountains occasionally with a cloth; and, (i) sweeps, mops and waxes hallways once per month. Mr. Massey receives assistance from: (a) his wife, who assures the girls' toilets and restrooms are clean; and, (b) teachers, who daily sweep their classrooms and empty their classroom trashcans into the hallway trashcans.

Discussion

1. Based on Trina's gathered data, which custodial services should be continued? Why? Which should be eliminated, and why?
2. Are there other custodial services that aren't mentioned that should be added? Why?

Improving Special Needs Students' Achievement Levels

Case

Stan Spaulding is completing his second year as the special education supervisor at Long Shore School District. He senses a need for professional development for the special education teachers after assessing the special education program. According to his data, the program's students do not appear to be achieving as specified on their Individual Education Plans (IEPs).

Discussion

1. How could Mr. Spaulding verify his assessment of the program?
2. How could Mr. Spaulding discern the specific professional development needed for his program's teachers?
3. What could Mr. Spaulding use to motivate the teachers to receive additional skill training.
4. List your plan of action for dealing with this scenario.

Improving Student Attendance

Case

Damon Dupree is the new assistant principal at Lakeside Middle School. A recent faculty survey indicates that student attendance is their major concern. Damon's first official duty is to investigate this situation and report back his findings to the principal.

Discussion

1. How can Damon determine if an attendance problem really exists? What constitutes an attendance problem?
2. What reporting procedures will Damon have to learn about? How can the current system's ways of reporting absences affect attendance? What about the process for accounting for tardy students? How about early dismissals?
3. How can parents help if the school opts to develop a campaign to improve attendance? How can teachers help?
4. What kind of incentive /award programs could be implemented? Do they work? Why or why not?
5. What would be different about this situation if was happening at an elementary school? How would things be different with secondary students? Bus riders compared to those secondary students who drive themselves to school?

Increasing Public Support of Education

Case

Hannah Hamilton, superintendent of Crosscreek Community School District, is concerned by what she perceives to be public apathy toward the school district. Few community members demonstrate much interest in public education, and business leaders complain that the only time they hear from school officials is during tax levy campaigns. Many community members question why educators keep asking for property tax increases and further financial aid. Hannah does not understand why more community members do not attend the public Board of Education meetings. The local paper reports short summaries of board proceedings, but few readers seem interested in those reports. Ms. Hamilton wants more public involvement in the schools so that they will understand the need for increased funding for maintaining and improving academic offerings and physical facilities.

Discussion

1. What appears to be the problem here? Why?
2. What is the role of the individual schools? The parents?
3. Would a district newsletter help?
4. Who would write it? What should be the topic? What format?
5. Is this a case of bad public relations? Is it more complicated than that? Explain.

Initiating Supervisory Functions

Case

The Chesterton School District recently hired Deborah Downing as its new instructional supervisor. The district consists of a high school, a middle school, and two elementary schools. As she settles into her new surroundings, she discovers that very few supervisory functions have occurred during her predecessor's tenure. Information gleaned from multiple sources indicates that instead of visiting schools, the former supervisor typically opted to remain in his office except for high profile public events. Further investigation yields no formal testing programs or supervisory plans for any of the district's schools. As a matter of fact, there are no records of any kind.

Discussion

1. Who could help Ms. Downing with this dilemma?
2. What action could Ms. Downing take for beginning supervision within this district?
3. What attitude could Deborah take upon entering the schools? What kind of reception could she expect to receive?
4. What role(s) could the building principals take to help Deborah initiate her instructional supervision duties?

Leaving a Special Education Classroom Unattended

Case

Keith Kirkland, a special education teacher at Cedar Lane High School, stepped out of his classroom to get a drink of water. On his way to the water fountain, Mr. Kirkland stopped two male students and asked them for a hall pass. Neither student could produce the necessary document so he ordered them to go the office to get a tardy slip.

As he bent to get his awaited drink, he heard a shrill shriek come from his open classroom door down the hall. He quickly raced back to his classroom to find five of his students huddled around Melissa Manning. She appeared to be quite upset as she had her jacket hood pulled up covering her head and Mr. Kirkland could hear her sobbing across the room.

"What's wrong?" queries Keith to the students surrounding Melissa. One student replies, "We're not sure, but she keeps saying something about keeping Dominic away from her." Mr. Kirkland places his hand on Melissa's shoulder, and she immediately starts flailing her arms as if she is defending herself. He says, "Whoa, Melissa, it's me, Mr. Kirkland. What's wrong?" She stops her physical movements, but her crying continues. Through her nonstop sobbing she squeaks out, "Dominic stuck that wet thing in my ear when you weren't in the room!" Keith looks over at Dominic Dunsworth, who is crouched down in his seat, across the room from Melissa. Several students indicate to Mr. Kirkland that Dominic was wandering around the room earlier, and others claim they didn't see anything.

Discussion

1. Could Mr. Kirkland be in trouble for going to get a drink of water?
2. Should teachers leave special education students unsupervised? Explain your answer.
3. Should Mr. Kirkland keep investigating this matter? Why or why not?

Locating a Missing Child

Case

Laverne Landon, principal at Parkside Elementary School, receives a telephone call from a frantic mother, Christine Craig. It is past 4:30 P.M., and Christine's 5-year old daughter, Caitlyn, is not home yet. Caitlyn's bus went by the house at the usual time, 4:00 P.M., but the child did not get off the bus. Ms. Craig questioned other children getting off the bus, but they had not seen Caitlyn. A subsequent neighborhood canvass did not net positive results. Ms. Landon detects on the phone that Ms. Craig is getting progressively more upset and is nearing hysteria. "What are you going to do about finding my little girl? Should I call the police? Or, maybe you should call them." wails Ms. Craig. She adds, "My sister and brother-in-law are going to pick me up and bring me and my mom and dad to school." Laverne Landon's mind is racing as she seeks the appropriate response for Ms. Craig.

Discussion

1. What actions should Laverne Landon take?
2. Are there some things that Ms. Landon can tell the parent?
3. What can the transportation department or bus service do to help?
4. Should the police be called? How should this be handled as far as the parent is concerned?

Maintaining Harmony Among Faculty

Case

Sharla Schwartz was recently hired as a reading teacher at Starr Middle School. Sharla's creativity and enthusiastic attitude about teaching children impresses the principal, Latrice Leonard. Instead of students only reading grade level texts, Sharla allows them to read books from any level they can comprehend. Her students appear to be performing well and are excited about their classes. Last week, Latrice received several comments from parents indicating their pleasure with Sharla's teaching approaches with their children and how impressed they were with the academic gains they have observed at home.

Ms. Schwartz came into Ms Leonard's office today visibly upset. "I don't know how to handle this situation," mutters Sharla as she plops down into the chair in front of Latrice's desk. Latrice looks over her reading glasses and asks, "What situation?" Sharla describes an encounter she and the upper grade level teachers had yesterday about the school's reading program. "They said I was ruining their reading programs because the children are reading all of the 'good books' before the students get to the grade levels where they teach. Furthermore, they implied that I was trying to make them look like bad teachers." Sharla finishes her story by saying, "I think they are just jealous."

Upon hearing Ms. Schwartz's last remark, Ms. Leonard raises her eyebrows, and says, "I don't doubt that, but how do you see resolving this situation?" Sharla half-heartedly replies, "Perhaps I should just dumb down my reading program."

Discussion

1. If you were Ms. Leonard what would you now say to Ms. Schwartz?
2. How could Ms. Leonard determine what is going on without making things worse?

3. Is this type of problem to be expected in educational administration? Or is this an isolated "personality" conflict?
4. Should Ms Leonard seek help from central office personnel? Or would she be seen as an administrator who cannot solve her own problems?
5. Should personality conflicts or disputes (sometimes called "dirty laundry") be aired? Or should they be covered up?

Making Pupil Assignment Decisions

Case

Felix and Frank Frederick attend Willow Bend Elementary School. Felix is a 5th grader, and Frank is in the 2nd grade. The Westwood Schools' board of education recently adopted a reassignment plan sending the 4th through 6th grades at Willow Bend Elementary to Whispering Meadows Elementary School, located ten miles away. The former 4th through 6th grade classrooms at Willow Bend are currently being used to house overflow student s from the adjacent, overcrowded Westwood High School. The Fredericks are upset because Felix walked his younger brother to school each day, and they feel that it is inappropriate for high school students to be in a building designed for elementary-age students.

Discussion

1. Do you think the Westwood school board should have the sole authority to make such pupil assignment decisions? Why or why not?
2. Do you think the Fredericks have any legal recourse at this point? Why?
3. Were there better tactics that could have been utilized in this case? What approach would you take?

Managing Maintenance Personnel

Case

Mack Melton, the head custodian at Creek Crossing Elementary School, approaches the building principal, Nancy Noland. He reports that he and his staff (two other middle-aged males and a younger adult female) find it difficult to complete their daily routines due to constant interruptions. Teachers stop the custodians in the halls and ask for favors, primarily odd jobs needing to be done in their classrooms. The most recent requests included: (a) changing light bulbs; (b) re-attaching a bulletin board to a wall; (c) trying to get a computer to work properly; (d) unloading refreshments from a teacher's car; (e) attempting to reset a clock to the correct time; and (f) adjusting a student desk to a comfortable height.

Ms. Noland nods her head as Mack recites the list. Simultaneously, she reflects back on a recent faculty meeting where the faculty voiced several complaints lodged against the building's custodial staff. Their complaints included irregularly emptied trash containers and infrequently swept and vacuumed floors.

Discussion

1. What should Ms. Noland do about the custodians' complaints?
2. What should Ms. Noland do about the teachers' complaints?

Mandating School Uniforms

Case

The Principal Advisory Council (PAC) at Winding Way Elementary School proposes to Principal Patty Peterson a school policy adopting mandatory school uniforms. This advisory council is composed of teachers, auxiliary staff, parents, administrators, and community representatives from the Winding Way attendance zone. They have carefully studied the issue and they believe that school uniforms would help alleviate the existing disparities between students, especially those from the newer affluent subdivisions and those from the government-supported housing areas.

According to the PAC proposal, the lower economic status children feel compelled to dress in the designer clothing styles worn by the upper income children. At this point in their lives, the students do not want to be "different," they desire to look like their peers. The PAC proposal rationale continues to explain that if the less affluent children do not "look" like the more affluent students, the lower income students' self esteems are harmed, they are distracted from their school studies, and they do not achieve their full potential. As Ms. Peterson finishes reading the proposal, her initial reaction is that she fears uniforms eliminate students' self-expression and creativity.

Discussion

1. How could Ms. Peterson handle the PAC's proposal regarding school uniforms?
2. Is Ms. Peterson's fear about school uniforms potentially eliminating self-expression and creativity a valid one? Why or why not?
3. What are some pros and cons associated with school uniforms?
4. Is there a middle ground in this issue? How could it be achieved?

Mentoring New Teachers

Case

The Principal's Advisory Committee at Spring Valley Elementary School, along with Principal Penny Price, unanimously opted to hire Samantha Smith as the new first grade teacher. Ms. Smith was excited about getting her first job, especially at Spring Valley. When she interviewed for this job, she learned that the Spring Valley faculty recently implemented many new curricular programs and that they had an innovative professional development program.

Ms. Price assigned a veteran first grade teacher, Melinda Morton, to mentor Samantha. However, as the school year progressed, Ms. Smith became frustrated and discouraged. She worked hard, but Ms. Morton gave her no guidance and very little orientation to the school and its culture. At times it appeared Melinda withheld important information from Samantha about the first grade instructional program.

Being a first year teacher, Samantha was reluctant to share her frustrations with anyone, especially Ms. Morton or Ms. Price. Samantha wanted to prove she was an excellent teacher, yet she felt very uncomfortable with the school culture and the new first grade curriculum. She completed her first year feeling good about her students and their learning, but she felt that her mentoring experience was seriously lacking.

Discussion

1. If you were Penny Price, how would you assure all new faculty members are being mentored properly?
2. What criteria would you use in selecting mentors for new faculty?
3. Create a list of key mentoring issues that you would review with prospective mentors. Explain your answers.
4. If you became aware of the situation in this case study, what steps would you take to deal with the dilemma?

Merging Two Rival Schools

Case

The Loveland Unified School District Board of Education resolved last spring to merge two rival middle schools and hired Ron Ronaldson as the new principal. Northside Middle School had sufficient room to absorb both the faculty and students from Southside Middle School. It is early July, and Ron is preparing for the upcoming school year. He is aware of two facts: (1) historically, the rivalry between the two schools has been quite intense, especially in sporting events; and, (2) many parents at both schools opposed the merger, and have been quite vocal with their objections.

Discussion

1. What actions should Ron take at this point?
2. How can a smooth transition be facilitated?
3. Who should be involved?
4. What roles do the following groups play in the merger: parents, teachers, students, classified staff, and community?

Minimizing Teaching Interruptions

Case

Gary Graves, the principal at Sycamore Junior High School, noted the following discussion items during a recent informal meeting with new teachers. These were some of the teachers' complaints: (a) an excessive noise level from a neighboring teacher's room; (b) students continually passing gas; (c) too few teacher parking places, especially when parents occupy the spaces while dropping off their children; and, (d) students released late from a teacher's class, thus making them tardy for their next class; (e) students chewing gum after gym class. The gym teachers allow students to chew gum, but gum chewing is not allowed throughout the remainder of the building; (f) the students carry many unauthorized items in their book bags (i.e., cell phones, pagers, electronic games). The teachers find it very difficult to prevent forbidden items when they are hidden away in the book bags; and (g) several students are habitually tardy due to their parents dropping them off late for school each morning.

Discussion

1. Help Mr. Graves place the items in order of importance and decide how to deal with each one.
2. Are there any items that the teachers should resolve without Mr. Graves' help?
3. Are there any items that are not worth worrying about? Explain

Minimizing the Effects of a Transient Student Population

Case

As the principal of a mid-sized junior high school, Alberta Ramirez is concerned about the number of students moving out of her building prior to the first grading period's end. The pumpkin harvest concludes in late September, prompting many migratory families to move on to other farming communities in search of work. While these families move out, other families move in, as transfers at the nearby military base affect other families. A recurring joke among the Rio Blanco Junior High School staff is to mark student names in pencil because they are not there long enough for ink to dry. The constant student population flux has the faculty concerned. The teachers contend they hardly know their students, and they strongly believe that student learning is adversely impacted by such transient lifestyles.

Discussion

1. How could Ms. Ramirez approach this problem?
2. What kind of solution could Ms. Ramirez present for the problem to the central office?
3. How could the course of study be revised to make provisions for the circumstances?
4. How could Ms. Ramirez involve the teachers in planning to meet the needs of the students?
5. What kind of evaluation system could be used to test the efficacy of your program?

Missing Curriculum Guides

Case

Candice Carlsen, a new first grade teacher at Glendening Elementary School, was excited about the possibilities of her teaching assignment. The scents of freshly painted walls and new carpeting enhanced her awareness that she was beginning her career in the building's newest wing. This factoid was the only useful information Candice gleaned from the required new staff orientation session she attended two days ago.

Principal Mel Matthews took Ms. Carlsen and a recently hired third grade teaching aide on a ten-minute tour of the campus before Mr. Matthews received a page reminding him he was supposed to be at an administrators meeting in the Rolling Plains School District's central office. As Mr. Matthews excused himself from the duo, Ms. Carlsen asked, "Oh, Mr. Matthews, when will I get a copy of the first grade curriculum guide?" Mr. Matthews replied, "Good question. I'll have someone try to find one for you. By the way, we realized yesterday that we were out of faculty handbooks, so you'll be getting your copies of those later," as he scurried out the door to the faculty parking lot. The two new employees looked at each other, shrugged their shoulders, and went to their respective classrooms.

While working in her classroom, Candice heard someone rustling around in the adjacent classroom. She went next door and introduced herself to one of the other four first grade teachers. Olive O'Bannon, a twenty-year veteran of Rolling Plains schools, said, "I'm glad to finally meet you. The other teachers and I met last week and you need to sign these letters we send home with the students. By the way, we agreed to start the year off as usual with our bear unit and you will need to bring iced bear cookies for your class. Ms. Reed chose red icing, Ms. Green, of course, chose green icing, I will do blue icing, so you choose a color for yours." When Candice finished signing the last letter, she asked, "Where can I get a copy of the first grade curriculum guide?" "Oh honey, mine is at home and I know it's not the most current version. Check the other teachers or downtown to see if they have one you can have," replied Ms. O'Bannon.

Discussion

1. What problems do you see in this scenario?
2. What could Mr. Matthews do for a better new staff orientation?
3. What would you be thinking if you were Ms. Carlsen?
4. What information is essential for new staff to have? How should this information be conveyed?

Monitoring Locker Rooms

Case

Rocky Reuben, an eighth grade physical education teacher, confronts Lakefront Junior High School's principal, Henry Hilton, with a dilemma. "You know I can't be two places at once, Mr. Hilton," comments Rocky. Mr. Hilton says, "What do you mean?" "I'm talking about trying to monitor student behavior at the end of P.E. class," replies Rocky. He continues, "The boys' and girls' dressing rooms are in two different areas of the gym, and I cannot oversee each one at the same time. At this age, I'm afraid that either group could get into a scuffle or hurt someone while horse playing, and I really don't want a lawsuit on my hands if an accident happens."

Discussion

1. What could Mr. Hilton suggest Mr. Reubens do?
2. Who is responsible if injuries occur during a fight or horseplay?
3. Is this kind of problem to be expected with junior high students?
4. Outline how you would suggest Mr. Hilton resolve this situation.

Observing Student-Initiated Segregation

Case

Donna Dodson is the principal of Central Junior High School, a racially diverse setting located in an urban district. During cafeteria duty, Donna notes that groups of white students are sitting at tables with only other white students. She observes the same behavior among other racial groups as well. The assistant principal, Aaron Adams, adds that most students seem to socialize with students from their own neighborhoods, and since most students are from "same race" neighborhoods, they tend to isolate themselves into "like" racial groups while in the cafeteria.

Discussion

1. Is there a problem here? Why or why not?
2. What could Donna or Aaron do about the situation?
3. Who could be of assistance in this matter?
4. What role do the students have in all of this?

Overemphasizing High School Football

Case

The press box stadium banner declaring "The Home of the Class 3A State Football Champions" glows after each Battling Blue Bears victory. Bright spotlights illuminate the sign's brilliant blue and white lettering that can be seen several blocks away from the gridiron where generations of Brandenburg High School alumni defended its gloried past. A string of numbers beneath the icon's text represent the successful campaigns that brought the prized state title to this proud community. To the local citizenry, football games are not simply sporting events; these games are a major entertainment outlet.

Football revenues support all of the school's sports teams' expenses. Recent football teams have not mirrored their predecessors' accomplishments, but the games are still well attended by parents and alumni in hopes of stirring another stellar year. Grumblings from discontented fans are pressuring school administrators to make changes to the struggling athletics program. The current administration does not favor such an overbearing emphasis on athletic prowess, but desires to highlight academic achievement instead.

Discussion

1. In this case, is football really receiving too much emphasis?
2. Who is to blame? Why?
3. Give suggestions for solving any dilemma seen here.
4. What role does the principal play in this case? Teachers? Athletic director?
5. Describe any overemphasis of a particular area in your school.

Planning Effective Faculty Meetings

Case

It's early January, and Helen Humphrey, principal at Mesa Verde Middle School, is disappointed with her faculty meetings to date. Originally, she envisioned mid-monthly meetings where she and the faculty could exchange timely administrative and instructional information. However, to date, these meetings tended to be disastrous.

For example, at September's meeting Ms. Humphrey presented a scholarly lecture on student achievement, but it was not well received by the faculty. The faculty feedback indicated that Helen only presented various theories concerning pre-adolescent developmental characteristics, but little or no practical application of those theories for their classroom settings. The Indian summer swelter highlighted the cafeteria's lack of air conditioning, and the overhead projector's bulb burst midway through her two-hour presentation.

October's meeting found her not prepared at all. To compensate for her ill preparation, Helen announced that it was an "open forum" meeting without a prescribed agenda. This action resulted in a barrage of complaints, which included: inadequate reserved parking spaces for teachers, inedible cafeteria food, excessive student tardies, insufficient coffee funds, inconsistent access to the Internet, frequent computer server "down time," and the ultimate barb, an apparent lack of building-level leadership. This meeting seemed interminable in spite of it lasting only an hour and a half.

The November meeting was cancelled, and the December meeting was another dismal failure. Ms Stevens, in an attempt to counter the October meeting's affront to her leadership efforts, compiled a record of errors and omissions made by each teacher, and she distributed that data to the respective teachers toward the end of the meeting. At this point, the meeting turned into a riotous debate with the principal on the defensive most of the time. Helen abruptly adjourned the meeting when she realized most of the faculty already left.

Helen, still reeling from the December meeting, prepares for the upcoming January faculty meeting. With this bleak history of meetings in mind, she is tempted to limit the next meeting to making standard announcements and handling routine procedures.

Discussion

1. List the chief criticisms of the principal's handling of the meetings.
2. What are the advantages of having teachers' meetings at all?
3. When, and by whom, should a yearly program of teachers' meetings be prepared?
4. Can, or should, faculty meetings ever be considered open forums?
5. What are faculty meetings like in your school? Describe one.

Pledging to the American Flag

Case

A student upsets Rose Richards, a 5th grade teacher at Revere Elementary School. The student, Bradley Botkins, refuses to salute or pledge allegiance to the American flag as a part of the class' morning routines. The Botkins agree with their son's refusal explaining that saluting and pledging offend sincerely held religious beliefs. Ms. Richards accepts the Botkins explanations, but now finds that other students are also refusing to participate in the saluting or pledging the flag.

Discussion

1. Is the refusal to salute due to sincerely held religious belief valid?
2. What can be done about the others in the class now refusing to participate?

Praying at Football Games

Case

Four games into the Western Hills High School football season, Paul Peterson, a junior student, approaches the school's principal, Randall Rebstock. Paul informs Mr. Rebstock that he objects to the traditional prayer being announced over the stadium's sound system prior to the kickoff at each game. The student further explains that he is agnostic and that he feels that the announced prayer at a public school function violates the separation of church and state.

Mr. Rebstock realizes that his fellow church deacons and numerous other citizens of this conservative community will notice the prayer's absence if the practice is immediately discontinued at this point in the season. To further complicate this dilemma, Paul Peterson indicates that he will contact the American Civil Liberties Union (ACLU) if the pre-game prayers continue.

Discussion

1. Should Randall Rebstock regard this as a legitimate concern? Explain your answer.
2. What are some viable alternatives for the principal to consider?
3. Does the pre-game prayer constitute being an essential portion of this event's purpose? Why or why not?
4. What are some possible complications for Randall if he ignores the Paul's complaint? What are some possible complications for Randall if he ceases the pre-game prayers?

Preparing an Integrated Instructional Unit

Case

Christine Cranston, the seventh grade level chair at Fairfield Junior High School, prepares to address some questions posed by some of her colleagues. Four of the seven teachers in her grade level prepare a curricular proposal and they need some help. Their proposal reflects their desire to integrate their subjects into a unified instructional unit. After several brainstorming meetings between the seventh grade math, reading, physical education, and social studies teachers, they conclude their unit's theme will be "The Rocky Mountains." They want the unit to last during a nine-week period of time, and to culminate with the students and teachers taking a field trip to the Rocky Mountains. The teachers' proposal ends with the questions below. If you were Ms. Cranston, how would you address these?

Discussion

1. How can we integrate our classes to make the unit more powerful?
2. What approach do you recommend for planning this unit?
3. How can our culminating activity, a field trip to the Rocky Mountains, become a reality?

Preparing for Parent-Teacher Conferences

Case

Over steaming cups of espresso, Heather and Hunter Hilton, fifth-grade parents at Belmont Elementary School, reflect on the parent-teacher conference they just concluded with their son's teacher, Katy Keller. Their son, Heath, brought home his first grading period's report card yesterday indicating the following grades:

Reading	A
Writing	B
Social Studies	A
Science	A
Mathematics	C
Art	A
Music	A
Physical Education	A

Both parents were pleased with all of Heath's efforts in all his academics, but they were concerned about mathematics. Mr. and Mrs. Hilton anticipated that today's twenty-minute conference with Ms. Keller would clarify what help Heath needed to improve his marks in math.

The conference started promptly at 7:30 A.M., the time that the Hiltons reserved during the previous Meet the Teacher orientation in late August. On this crisp early November morning, Ms. Keller greeted the Hiltons with a warm handshake and a hardy smile. She proceeded to direct them to a kidney-shaped table, where she sat across from the visiting parents. Katy initiated the conference by appraising Heather and Hunter of Heath's deportment, his leadership abilities in cooperative learning activities, and his insatiable appetite for reading materials atypical of most his peers. The teacher praised the parents for exposing Heath to the fine arts and how he incorporates his visual, theatrical, and musical experiences into his journal writings and classroom discussions.

Samples of Heath's work were showcased in a portfolio Ms. Keller opened midway through the conference. The Hiltons shuffled through various reading, writing, mathematics, social studies, and science assignments completed by Heath since the onset of school. The parents noted the authenticity of the displayed work from their son's penmanship and his occasional lack of attention to details, such as dotting and crossing particular letters and ending sentences with appropriate punctuation marks. All artifacts were labeled with bright red A's or A minuses and were noticeably devoid of many teacher corrections, as expected for that caliber of work. Following the scan through Heath's portfolio, Katy brought the meeting to closure by informing the Hiltons if they had any further questions about Heath's progress to write, email, or phone her at school.

The Hiltons left the conference feeling good about their son's fifth grade experiences thus far. Now that they are debriefing between themselves the events of less than a half-hour ago, Hunter Hilton peers over the large ceramic cup he embraces in his hands, as he remarks to his wife, "Honey, you know I'm pleased with Heath's work this year, but did you see or hear any reasons why he had a C in math on his report card?" "Ah, you're right. The papers were all A's and Ms. Keller didn't say anything about Heath's math efforts," replied Heather as she downed the last drop of her morning brew. At this point, the Hiltons were confused by the apparent disconnect between their son's displayed work and the grade on his report card.

Discussion

1. What were the positive attributes of the depicted parent-teacher conference?
2. How could Ms. Keller better prepare for future parent-teacher conferences?
3. Obviously, the Hiltons will contact Ms. Keller. How could she respond to their concerns about Heath's math efforts?

Preventing Plagiarism

Case

Dora Dansfield, the twelfth-grade English teacher at Bainesville High School, peers at the stack of senior research papers perilously perched on the bookshelf adjacent to her desk. This project is the traditional culminating activity in her senior-level class. The students spend countless hours toiling to meet the rigorous expectations Ms. Dansfield details. Past students submitted multiple drafts of their papers for preliminary approval, but this year's crew was unlike their predecessors, as they are quite adept at research writing. Dora suspects the batch of papers awaiting her review will rank as among the best in her twenty-five year career.

Dora was particularly proud of this year's graduating class. Her son, Darren, and several of his closest friends are departing their alma mater as honor graduates. Darren's best friend, Paul Preston, was recently named class valedictorian, edging out Darren for this honor by only thousandths of a point. Not only does the class valedictorian receive a substantial scholarship to attend a prestigious private university, but also the recipient delivers the commencement speech. Darren is understandably disappointed, as he knows his mother, as a single parent, cannot afford to support his two siblings and send him to the university of his dreams. He resolves to supplement his higher education pursuits through part-time employment and student loans.

After skimming the uppermost paper off the stack, Ms. Dansfield scans the cover page noting its title and then its author, Paul Preston. She silently chuckles, as she is not surprised that his paper was the last one submitted. Paul chronically procrastinates, yet expects perfection from his efforts. Even though Dora is accustomed to spending many hours grading the senior research papers, this year she adds a new twist to the project's evaluation. After checking the papers' mechanics, Ms. Dansfield will subject them to a new technology subscription service that detects probable plagiarism. This subscription is in response to the district's school board wanting to stringently enforce a zero-tolerance policy against plagiarism.

Dora receives the plagiarism scanning service's report within a matter of hours. A cursory scan reveals that only one student's paper was suspect, Paul Preston's. She is shocked, and suspects a mistake; however, the report specifically cites significantly large portions of Paul's project text were copied verbatim from a variety of scholarly journals. Dora is sickened by the news and is torn about what to do about this dilemma. Disclosing the plagiarism violation to school authorities could strip Paul of his valedictorian designation. Furthermore, if this happens, Darren will replace Paul and subsequently receive the scholarship to the school of his dreams.

Discussion

1. What are some viable options for Ms. Dansfield in handling this situation?
2. What are the positives and negatives associated with the options mentioned in Question 1?
3. Who should be involved in resolving this dilemma? Explain your answer(s).

Preventing Potential Internet Abuse

Case

"Oh, no! Come here quick, Ms. Hammonds!" screams Britney Brown, covering her eyes and quickly spinning her chair 180 degrees. Helen Hammonds, the Edison High School librarian, rushes to Britney's rescue at her computer. "What's the matter?" queries Helen. "Look at what's on this screen. I sat down at this computer and that's what was already there," mutters a disgusted and embarrassed Britney. Helen understands Britney's reactions as she sees firsthand the multiple flashing images of tattoos and jewelry adorning almost every human body part imaginable. Ms. Hammonds, attempting to console the flustered student, says, "Go over to one of the other computers as I handle this matter."

The shell-shocked student scampers to another terminal while Ms. Hammonds records which computer, the time of day, the website's URL, and the student involved. Seeing Ms. Hammonds write her name, Britney asks, "I'm not going to be on report, am I?" "This is our standard procedure, Britney. I turn this information in to the office and they sift through it," replies Ms. Hammonds. As Helen completes recording the requisite information, another student, Chad Connors, and his health and fitness instructor, Steve Stoneberger, rush into the library toward the computer in question.

The incoming student and teacher are panting as they had obviously taken fast strides upstairs. "Oh, Ms. Hammonds," gasps Chad, "I see you found what I did." While the student catches his breath, Mr. Stoneberger explains that Chad was doing research for him on the potential health risks of tattoos and body piercings for a class discussion when he encountered the questionable website. Chad explains further, "The initial site I went to was tame and didn't have the information I was looking for, so I cancelled that screen. The next thing I know, this new pop-up screen appears that I can't get rid of. I looked around for you, Ms. Hammonds, but you weren't around. I wanted someone to know that I didn't intentionally access that site, so that's when I rushed downstairs to get Mr. Stoneberger. I guess I wasn't fast enough, huh?" "I don't think Coach Stoneberger is going to recruit you for the track team, Chad," chided Britney as she further quipped, "I hope his name goes on that report, too."

Discussion

1. What should Ms. Hammonds and Mr. Stoneberger do about this unfortunate incident?
2. What is your school's policy regarding Internet use?
3. Does it appear that there are sufficient safeguards in place to protect students from accessing potentially offensive websites? Explain your answer.

Preventing School Personnel From Using Others' Personal Materials

Case

"That's the final straw!" exclaims Carlen Christian as she scrambles through her desk drawer searching for a pen. Ben Beedy, the high school principal, asks, "What's wrong, Ms. Christian?" Carlen slams the desk drawer and huffs, "Mr. B., the teachers use my phone to make calls, they pillage through my desk, and they steal my personal pens and note pads without giving these actions a second thought." Mr. Beedy says, "I've never seen them do those things, but I'll take your word for it."

Discussion

1. What can be done to alleviate this problem?
2. Who should be involved in the solution?

Prioritizing School Administrator Professional Development Activities

Case

Central office supervisors in the Water Valley School District discuss the upcoming year's administrator professional development activities. They brainstorm and derive the following potential topics:

School Climate	Open Houses
Parent-Teacher Organizations	Food Service
Curriculum Design	Student Teachers
Student Altercations	Student Lockers
Block Scheduling	Technology
Parent-School Relations	Media Relations
School Guidance	Site-Based Decision-Making
Legal Issues	Textbook Selection
School Sponsored Events	Staff Personnel
Teacher Evaluations	Safety Drills
Parent/Community Volunteers	Gang Prevention
Campus-Level Report Cards	School Health Program
Campus Discipline Plans	Science Fairs
Budgeting	Transportation
Classified Personnel	Student Organizations
School Assemblies	Substitute Teachers
Vandalism	Standardized Testing
Maintenance	Student Dress Code

Discussion

1. Narrow and prioritize the list to the ten most important topics for the district's administrative team. Describe how you would go about doing this.
2. Separate and prioritize the list into three different lists; early elementary,

middle school and secondary school. Are the most important concerns the same for all levels?
3. If this was your district, should any areas of concern be added? If yes, what?
4. How would the list change if professional development activities were being planned for teachers instead of principals?

Prioritizing Teacher Requests

Case

Shannon Sherman, the principal at Eastgate Elementary School, received the following individually written requests from teachers. The teachers are seeking permission to: (a) use a teacher-made math textbook in lieu of the school purchased math textbook; (b) conduct a class project fundraiser; either a bake sale or garage sale; (c) hold an assembly for all of the 6th grade social studies classes and invite a prominent gay rights activist as the guest speaker; and, (d) have a party for each major holiday in the teachers homeroom: Halloween, Thanksgiving, Christmas, Valentine's Day, Easter and Earth Day.

Discussion

1. If you were Ms. Sherman, prepare a response to each request and give a rationale for your decisions.
2. What other requests are administrators likely to receive from teachers?

Promoting a Proposed Administrator Evaluation System

Case

One of the duties assumed by the new superintendent at West Central School District is to implement a merit pay plan for the administrative team. Dr. Wesley Woodman desires to initiate an incentive plan correlated to administrative job performance, going beyond the current percentage rate pay increase system. Tying the administrators' possible pay increases to their annual evaluations would be a new twist to the pay plan.

The district's administrators have gathered at the central office where Dr. Woodman will present the new merit pay system. Word has spread that a "pay-for-performance" system is on the drawing board. As Dr. Woodman begins the meeting, he senses the dissention among the administrative personnel.

Discussion

1. What tactic(s) could Dr. Woodman use to explain the new pay and evaluation procedure?
2. One of the first questions directed to Dr. Woodman by the administrators involves the fairness of a merit system. How could he ease their anxiety?
3. After Dr. Woodman's lengthy explanation and discussion about the new procedure, one administrator states that he refuses to be evaluated by this method, and leaves the meeting upset. The others turn to him and wait to see his reaction. What could Dr. Woodman say at this point to the administrative team? How could Dr. Woodman deal with the administrator who left the meeting?
4. If you initially had complete control of changing a traditional pay and evaluation system, what would you have done differently? Explain your answer.

Protecting Our Children

Case

Mack Morris found himself in the middle of a situation that school administrators hope they never have to face. As the principal at Van Buren High School, he is making split second decisions that could have life saving and/or threatening ramifications. Mr. Morris received a telephone call less than ten minutes ago informing him students armed with semi-automatic guns, grenades, and bombs would be descending upon the nearby Pierce Middle School. He immediately contacted the PMS principal, informing her of the threat, as well as making quick phone calls to the superintendent and the city police department. Mr. Morris knew his next move was to enact lockdown procedures at VBHS.

As he left his office to make the announcement, he bumped into Carolyn Campbell, a ninth-grade English teacher. "I'm sorry, Ms. Campbell," muttered Mr. Morris as he regained his bearings. "You look like you've seen a ghost, Mack," gasped Ms. Campbell when she saw Mack's ashen face. "There's been a terrorist threat made on Pierce, and we're about to go into lockdown mode here. I hope to goodness this is just a hoax," replied the harried principal. "Oh my, God!" shrieked Carolyn, "I've got to go get my precious Christy over at Pierce!" Before Mr. Morris could utter another word, Ms. Campbell darted out of the school office towards her minivan in the faculty parking lot.

Discussion

1. At this point, should Mr. Morris pursue Ms. Campbell, or should he make the lockdown announcement? Explain your answer?
2. Should Ms. Campbell be reprimanded for her actions? Why or why not?
3. What actions could Mr. Morris take to prevent similar responses from faculty in the future?

Rating Teachers on the Internet

Case

David Danbury is a parent of a student attending Washington Heights High School. He recently discovered his son, Dennis, working on a website for his technology class. While Mr. Danbury was pleased with the complex nature of the assigned project, he was disturbed by the website's content. The website's name is, "Rate Your Teacher," and it contains a series of questionable survey items pertaining to WHHS faculty. A few of the twenty-five sample questions include:

5. Do you think Coach Clark is sexy? Why or why not? Use one of the following languages for your answer: Latin, Spanish, French, German, or Klingon
8. Approximate Miss Stapleton's bra size. State your answer using: (a) U.S. and metric measurements, and (b) Arabic and Roman numerals.
9. What type of man is Principal Patterson? (a) boxers, (b) briefs, or (c) thong Explain your response.

Dennis claims that the website is for a unit in survey research using the Internet as a medium and the questions are strictly for fun. Mr. Danbury intends to contact the school principal to express his displeasure with this project.

Discussion

1. When Mr. Patterson receives the call from Mr. Danbury, to whom should Mr. Patterson be referred? Why?

2. Why do you think that Mr. Danbury is upset over this project?
3. What types of parameters should a technology project include?
4. Do you think Dennis Danbury should be reprimanded over this project? Why or why not?
5. Is Dennis protected by First Amendment rights? Why or why not?

Reducing the Cost of Education

Case

The Board of Education for Springdale Schools developed the following proposal for reducing school costs. Several bond issues to raise property taxes were recently rejected by the district's voters, thus prompting this cost-cutting list. As an educational consultant hired by the board, Daniel D'Amico is to make recommendations at their upcoming board meeting: (a) eliminate the office of superintendent of schools and assign his duties to the one high school principal and the two elementary school principals; (b) eliminate music, art, and P.E. classes at all levels; (c) increase all class sizes to 35 students per class; (d) eliminate the position of school librarian and distribute the duties to classroom teachers; (e) eliminate guidance counselors and distribute the duties to the building principals; (f) eliminate the position of assistant principal at all three campuses; (g) eliminate the services of the school nurses; (h) eliminate the clerical help in the superintendent's office; and, (i) discontinue the practice of furnishing students free textbooks and supplies.

Discussion

1. Which of the preceding proposals would you consider objectionable from the standpoint of the overall welfare of the students?
2. Which policies would you recommend be followed?
3. How can the Board determine what actually must be done?
4. What timeframe do you think they should work under?

Regulating Participation in Extracurricular Activities

Case

Rhonda Ross, the newly appointed principal at Manchester High School, smiles as she glances over the extracurricular activities listed in the school yearbook. There appears to be a wide variety of academic, athletic, student government, and fine arts offerings that have effectively enhanced the school's curriculum. As she closely examines each groups' membership she discovers that a highly distinguishable core of students hold a vast majority of each organization's principal positions. For example, the school newspaper editor is also the Spanish Club president, the basketball team captain, and appears to be actively involved in numerous other extracurricular activities.

Ms. Ross contacts the assistant principal, Luke Lee, and delegates him to research systems for regulating student participation in extracurricular activities. Mr. Lee finds two different systems: a "major/minor" format and a "point" system. Under the first system, activities are classified as either "major" or "minor" based on their importance and its expected workload. Standards regulate the number of major and minor activities in which a student participates. Under the "point" system, activities receive points based on predetermined criteria, and rules restrict the number of extracurricular points a student carries.

Ms. Ross now assigns Mr. Lee to convene an ad hoc committee to review both systems for the purpose of recommending one as suitable for Manchester High School.

Discussion

1. Who should serve on the review committee, and why is their participation important? Explain.
2. What are the objections to one student holding so many important positions? Explain.

3. Which system of regulating extracurricular participation do you prefer? Or, do you think a system is needed at all? Why?
4. If you were on the review committee, what recommendation(s) would you make? What additional rules, if any, would you propose to either system, if adopted?

Removing a Bad Reputation

Case

Sara Sandridge was excited about her assignment as Redbud Lane Elementary School's new fourth grade teacher. This was her first teaching job, and she knew she had what it took to be a success. Sara had a delightful experience as a fourth grade student teacher at another school and now she felt very prepared to take on the challenges of her very own classroom. Her initial zeal unfortunately fades as she faces the reality of her new position.

The fourth grade at Redbud Lane Elementary had been dominated for the past twenty years by an infamous duo, Madeline Masterson and Francis Fritz. They forged a solid reputation of intimidating students and running over parents, colleagues, and administrators. For example, Ms. Masterson was known for humiliating students in front of their peers if they gave wrong answers to her questions. One day a student came to school dirty, and Ms. Fritz proceeded to take the child to the locker room where she threw the child into a shower, clothes and all. Both teachers held their students to high academic standards and accepted no excuses for inferior work. Students performed to their expectations and passed, or struggled and failed. Theirs was a world of absolutes, and they thrived on convincing everyone that they were right and everyone else was wrong.

Ms. Fritz's retirement created the open position that Ms. Sandridge assumed. Ms. Masterson was up for retirement at year's end. Sara was unaware of the negativity associated with Redbud Lane's fourth grade until she encountered her students' parents on Open House night. She was greeted with parent comments such as, "I hope my child survives fourth grade," and "We know what this grade level is like, and we have to get it over with." Sara was confused by these comments until she conferred later with other colleagues about their underlying meanings. Ms. Sandridge realized that she was facing a double obstacle, establishing her own reputation as a teacher while attempting to diminish the poor reputation of her predecessor.

Discussion

1. What steps could Ms. Sandridge take to help her in this situation?
2. Who could Ms. Sandridge use as helpful resources? In what ways could these people help her?
3. Should Ms. Sandridge wait until Ms. Masterson retires before she does anything about the fourth grade's poor reputation? Why or why not?

Requiring School District Residency

Case

A recent Board of Education election for the Thomasville School District resulted in adding several new members to the board. Once seated, a new member, Nora Nathanielson, moved that teaching contracts be offered only to teachers who were actual school district residents and that all other teaching positions occupied by non-district dwellers be declared vacant. All resulting vacancies are to be filled using "local talent" or by permitting current non-resident teachers to move within the school district boundaries, thereby keeping their jobs. Superintendent Sam Stansel is not comfortable with this new policy because his home is located in Hallstown, an adjacent community to Thomasville.

Discussion

1. What action should the Sam Stansel take in securing teachers to fill the vacancies?
2. Is this a sound policy? Why or why not?
3. Should administrators be held to the same residency restrictions? Why or why not?

Requiring Teachers to Perform Additional Duties

Case

Lou Langston, a teacher at Dartmouth High School, recently determined that too much was being asked of her by the school's administrators. When Ms. Langston was hired last year, she and the remainder of the Dartmouth's faculty were assigned various extra duties. She now refuses to perform any of the following duties: (a) perform hall duty during passing period; (b) monitor bus loading/unloading one day per week; (c) monitor lunchroom activities after her lunch period; (d) decorate a hallway bulletin board for a two-week period during the school year; (e) attend the annual open house in the fall; (f) attend the report card night at the end of the first three grading periods; and, (g) check restrooms between classes.

Discussion

1. Are the Dartmouth teachers required to perform "extra" duties? Explain your answer.
2. Which are extra duties? Which activities are part of the job?
3. Does the teacher have grounds for a grievance? Why or why not?
4. Does the board have a case against the teacher if this goes to court?

Resolving Personality Conflicts

Case

Sally Snider, the secretary at Arlington Heights Middle School, takes her job very seriously. Lately though, new faculty members question if she "knows her place," as they feel she exceeds the limits of her school secretary position. These new teachers report that Sally demands explanation whenever teachers request supply items for their classrooms, and she acts like it is her money being dispensed when purchases are made. Ms. Snider allegedly refuses to allow some of the teachers any more paper stating they have already used up their quota. Other teachers report that Sally is being rude to parents and callers on the phone. Overall, the staff at Arlington Heights considers Ms. Snider to be just plain "bossy." Ron Roberts, the school principal, values Sally's competence, but he is concerned about overall school morale.

Discussion

1. How can Mr. Roberts handle this without making matters worse?
2. Is there a risk that confronting the secretary will result in making no one happy and alienating a very competent secretary? Explain.
3. How can these charges be verified?
4. Should the secretary be confronted? How? Told of her accusers? How?
5. Should the central office be made aware of the charges? Explain your answer.

Respecting the Assistant Principal

Case

It was a hot and humid day at the new Raleigh Middle School. Students and teachers were very uncomfortable due to the air conditioning not working properly. The building principal was at a conference all day; therefore, the assistant principal, Hal Hollums, was the only administrator at the school.

Several teachers came into the office at noon and told the secretary they would be leaving for the day. They indicated they were feeling sick due to the heat and humidity, and refused to continue working in the new building without air conditioning. When the office secretary informed Mr. Hollums of the teachers' decisions, he immediately ran to the parking lot and confronted the exiting teachers as they were getting in their cars. Hal demanded that the teachers return to their assigned duties, and he added that disciplinary measures would be taken against any teacher refusing to return. Three of the four teachers reluctantly acquiesced. The fourth teacher became very upset, and told Mr. Hollums he was leaving, and threatened he would hurt him if he tried to prevent him from leaving.

Discussion

1. Does Mr. Hollums, the assistant principal, have authority to demand teachers complete a full day of work? Why or why not?
2. When the principal leaves the building in your school, who is in charge?
3. Is a certified assistant administrator automatically the decision-maker and authority figure when the principal is not in the school? Explain your answer.
4. What parameters, if any, would you set for personnel put in charge of the school when the principal is away?

Respecting the Confidentiality of Special Needs Students

Case

Sally Smith, a special education teacher, would often have lunch with a friend and colleague, Betty Brooks, a third grade teacher, in the Highland Heights Elementary School teachers' lounge. On this particular day, Sally was venting her frustrations regarding Johnny Johnson, a special education student. Sally bemoaned to Betty the numerous lesson modifications that Johnny required as indicated in his Individual Education Plan (IEP). Carolyn Cross, an educational aide, overhears the conversation between the two teachers. Coincidentally, Carolyn is a neighbor of Jack and June Johnson, Johnny's parents.

One day, Carolyn was out in her yard raking leaves alongside her neighbors, the Johnsons. Carolyn mentions to the Johnsons that she had heard that their son, Johnny, was having some problems in school. When queried by Jack and June as to where she heard this information, Carolyn stated that she heard his special education teacher talking about his IEP to another teacher in the lounge. The Johnsons were furious at the thought of Johnny's teacher talking about him in that setting. They were even more upset at the possibility that more people may have heard this same conversation and that this talk about Johnny reflected negatively upon them as parents. The Johnsons immediately called the school principal to schedule a meeting regarding this situation.

Discussion

1. Should Sally have been discussing Johnny's situation in the teachers' lounge? Why or why not?
2. What are the legal ramifications of disclosing confidential information in a public place?

3. What should Carolyn have done with the information she overheard in the lounge?
4. Do Johnny's parents have right to be angry, or are they simply overreacting?
5. What should the principal do in this situation?

Revamping a Dysfunctional Grade-Level Team

Case

For the past three years, the six 7th grade teachers at Grandview Middle School continuously disagreed on curriculum, instruction, and grade level duty responsibilities. Instead of cooperating as a team, like the other two grade level teachers did, each 7th grade teacher refused to interact with others. At the onset of the school day, these teachers simply closed their classroom doors, and only interacted with their respective students. Teacher to teacher communication was virtually nonexistent. The principal, the other faculty, and even the students noticed the friction between these teachers.

Superintendent Tom Taft transferred Hal Hunter to Grandview because of Hal's leadership abilities. Mr. Hunter had a reputation throughout the district as a model teacher. Hal was assigned a vacant position within the seventh grade, due to a retirement. Principal Polly Parkinson was pleased with Mr. Hunter's assignment and made him the grade level chair. Hal reluctantly accepted the chair position, as he hoped he could bring change to the unproductive, non-communicative situation within Grandview's seventh grade teaching staff.

Discussion

1. Before students arrive for the new school year, Ms. Parkinson schedules grade level team meetings. Mr. Hunter needs an agenda for the meeting with the seventh grade teachers. What should be on this agenda?
2. What approach should Mr. Hunter take in handling the lack of communication between the teachers?
3. Polly Parkinson assumes what role in this situation?
4. If the problem continues after many attempts to improve the relationships, what could Mr. Hunter recommend for solving the unfortunate situation?

Revamping High School Graduation Ceremonies

Case

Ellen Elgar, the high school principal at Vinson High School, waves to the exiting custodial staff following their attempts to clean up the mess left by tonight's graduation participants. She ponders if there is something that can be done to avoid such an unruly display next year. Ms. Elgar remembers her high school graduation ceremony as a highly polished and dignified occasion, a far cry from what had occurred here only a few hours ago.

Tonight's graduates cart wheeled across the stage, threw confetti, sprayed silly string, and released pigeons at strategic times throughout their graduation ceremony. The attending parents and guests were not much more controlled than the outgoing senior class. Many in the audience ignored posted and verbal requests to remain seated throughout the ceremony. These unruly observers crammed into the aisles and charged toward the stage in their zeal to obtain pictures and video of this raucous event. Air horn blasts and whooping family members prevented more sedate attendees from hearing their honoree's names as they were announced.

Faculty attendance has gradually declined over the past several years as each ensuing senior class attempts to outperform their predecessors' shenanigans. A tear trickles down Ellen's cheek, and she shudders at the thought of reading the next few editions of the Johnson City Journal, the local daily paper. She anticipates there will be several letters to editor dedicated to this evening's activities.

Discussion

1. How can Ms. Elgar restore order to the graduation ceremonies?
2. Should graduation ceremonies reflect a more relaxed, celebratory atmosphere or a more staid, traditional air? Why?
3. Who could be involved in developing a plan to revise the graduation ceremonies? Justify your choices.

Reviewing an Open Campus Policy

Case

Ralph and Ramona Reddy's food stand, the Reddy Mart, serves Springdale Junior High School students quick, hot lunches. The Reddy family has operated this business in the same location, two blocks from campus, since 1960 when the current junior high school served as the district's high school. The establishment takes its patrons back to a simpler time and place with its diner-like atmosphere accented by bright red vinyl booths, shiny chrome accents, and a thumping corner jukebox. A flashing marquee upfront sports supportive messages to its most loyal patrons, the adolescent lunch crowd from SJHS.

The new SJHS principal, Patricia Pitman, ponders over various purported problems attributed to a lunchtime "open" campus policy. During their forty-minute lunch break, students are permitted to walk home, remain on campus, or as many opt, patronize the Reddy Mart. Some students bypass this traditional icon and scamper a half-mile farther to the new shopping plaza's food court where a variety of fast food chains have recently opened. These dining places offer many meal options including menus for health conscious individuals not available elsewhere. In order to get back in time for their class after lunch, students dining at the Springdale Plaza have been seen hitchhiking or recklessly scurrying back to campus.

Other problems associated with lunchtime and afterwards include: (a) neighborhood residents complaining about students loitering, littering, and vandalizing around their property; (b) reports of students smoking and possibly drinking in area alleys; (c) a high tardy rate for the beginning of sixth period, the period immediately following lunch; and, (d) afternoon-only truancies. The open campus policy has been in effect since the junior high moved into the former high school. Ms. Pitman believes this policy is outdated and other options need to be considered. She also realizes that the Reddys are already reeling from losing customers to the new food court, and a closed campus policy will undoubtedly force this long-time business to shutter its windows for good.

Discussion

1. What are some viable options for Ms. Pitman to consider?
2. Who could help Ms. Pitman with the problems associated with the open campus policy?
3. Should Ms. Pitman be concerned about the ramifications for the Reddy Mart? Why or why not?

Reviewing the Treasurer's Files

Case

Since the recent election, Nathan Nagy, a newly elected school board member, is seen each day at the River Falls School District's central office. He mainly visits the treasurer's files. The school treasurer, Damon Delaney, finds out from his secretary that Mr. Nagy mainly reviews district employees' personnel files. Mr. Delaney informs Dr. Margaret Medinger, the superintendent, about Nathan's frequent perusals through the personnel files and that he has been seen making copies of those files.

Discussion

1. Should Dr. Medinger approach the new board member concerning his daily activities of reviewing and copying personnel files? Why or why not?
2. What are the legal implications?
3. Dr. Medinger and Mr. Delaney sense there are many employees very upset about Mr. Nagy's file reviews. How will you address those with concerns?
4. Regardless of the legal implications, how do you personally feel about the situation? Why do you feel that way?

Revising a Teacher Sick Leave Policy

Case

The Peaceful Valley School District's Board of Education requests that Superintendent Stan Smitherman make recommendations toward revising the teachers' sick leave policy. Within this rural district, allegations contend that teachers abuse the current system. The present system allows fifteen days annually, and if unused, the remaining days can be applied toward early retirement. Stan and the Board want to provide the best possible policy for dealing with teacher absenteeism due to illness.

Discussion

1. If you were Stan, what kind of sick leave policy would you recommend?
2. Is the current sick leave policy satisfactory? Why or why not?
3. Consider the following sick leave policy elements. How would you recommend they be handled in your proposed policy?
    a. How should sick leave policies be administered?
    b. How should sick leave policies be enforced?
    c. What "call in sick" procedures should teachers use?
    d. What if a teacher shows up at school after calling in sick claiming that they "feel better" (after a substitute teacher has been called in)?
    e. Should teachers be charged with sick leave days when leaving school early for an illness?

Revising Teacher Employment Applications

Case

As the new principal at Rosewood Middle School, Roberta Silverman, searches the office file drawers for a teacher employment application. Roberta finally discovers some applications. The following is an outline of the application:

I. Personal data
    A. Name
    B. Address
    C. Phone
    D. Age
    E. Health
    F. Height and Weight
    G. Church attended
    H. Marital status
    I. Plans to have children
II. Education
    A. Degrees
    B. Certificates held
III. Experience
    A. Prior teaching experience
    B. Other employment
IV. References
V. Military Service
VI. Arrests and Convictions

Discussion

1. Which questions should be deleted?
2. What should be added?
3. What should the ideal application form contain?

Revising Teacher Observation Criteria

Case

Sarah Stallings, the new principal at Fox Valley High School, finds the following observation form in her office files. After looking over the form, she considers adopting it, but has not yet decided how to implement an observation program. Currently, there are no set procedures and the teachers do not seem to care one way or the other about the process.

Teacher Observation Form

Teacher: *Date of visit:*
Length of stay: *Period*

a. Did the lesson appear to be well planned? What was the topic being discussed?
b. Was enthusiasm evidenced in the teacher's presentation?
c. Were the students involved in the activities? Did they appear interested in the lesson?
d. Describe interactions between the teachers and students, and students with students.
e. Was there any unusual activity occurring?
f. Was there anything unusual about the physical appearance of the room?
g. Were personal qualities of the teacher positive? (speech, dress, grooming, etc.)?

Principal's suggestions and/or comments.

Discussion

1. What is required to evaluate effective teaching?
2. How can a system of evaluation be implemented?
3. Evaluate the short visit form. What could be added, and why? What could be deleted, and why?

Revising Teacher Transfer Policies

Case

Brenda Benson and Samantha Simpson, instructional supervisors for the Crestridge School District, discover there are problems regarding teacher transfers. Both supervisors found there was only a vague transfer policy of which only a few people were aware. This policy was based on past practices, but there does not appear to be an official written policy.

After interviewing several district personnel, Brenda and Samantha find it difficult to determine how the policy evolved. Teachers contend reassignments are arbitrary, as from their perspective principals rid their buildings of troublemakers by sending them to another campus across town. According to principals, the current policy forces weak teachers upon them. Summer reassignments are not known until shortly before school starts creating much angst among teachers and administrators. The superintendent contends that teacher transfers occur only to strengthen the receiving school or subject area by providing the best teacher possible.

Discussion

1. Is this a problem for the Crestridge School District? Why or why not? If it is a problem, should Brenda and Samantha ignore it? Why or why not?
2. Will teachers always complain about this type of thing? Explain your answer.
3. Does there need to be a formalized policy? Who should help craft one, if one is needed?
4. Who should be consulted before finalizing these types of actions?

Selecting High School Cheerleaders

Case

Cheerleaders at Riverview High School are traditionally selected each spring through auditions before the entire student body. Aspiring cheerleaders perform individual and group yells during tryouts conducted in the gymnasium. Following the tryouts, the student body votes by secret ballot according to whom they perceive to be the best representatives for their school. The top two vote receivers from each class (grades 9–12) become the cheerleading squad for the upcoming school year. Nick Northgate, the new Riverview High School principal, wants to investigate other ways of selecting the cheerleading squad.

Discussion

1. Who could Mr. Northgate consult for some viable options?
2. From your perspective, what are some viable options? Describe these options.
3. How could Mr. Northgate determine which viable options are best? Explain.

Selecting New Textbooks

Case

Beverly Barnes, the curriculum director at Union Valley School District, wants to form an ad hoc textbook committee. Their aim is to select a new language arts program for the district. The superintendent, Fern Farmington, believes that it's in the best interest of the students and teachers if the same publisher's texts are utilized through all the grade levels. Ms. Barnes does not support this belief. She contends that the language arts content standards should be supported by the best possible texts available, and those books may come from various publishers. The language arts teachers at Lee Middle School (grades 3–5) developed their own curriculum materials last year, because their former textbooks had completely fallen apart. The Grant High School English Department uses a curriculum they wrote when their department chair accepted his position two decades ago. Grant graduates often praise their language arts preparation as they claim it more than adequately prepares them for rigorous university-level work.

Discussion

1. Who should Ms. Barnes select to serve on the ad hoc textbook selection committee? Justify your selections.
2. List the criteria that the textbook committee could use in selecting their new texts.
3. Is a new language arts curriculum necessary? Why or why not?
4. Should the current curriculum be considered as a viable option? Why or why not?

Treating Student Athletes Equally

Case

In the latest edition of the Rio Blanco Reporter is the following letter to the editor:

Dear Editor:
Two years ago my tennis partner and I qualified for the regional tournament. We had an undefeated record going into the competition. Unfortunately, my partner failed a class, and could not compete with me at that tournament due to the state's "no pass, no play" rule. I was allowed to compete at the regional tournament with another female partner, but alas, we were defeated and subsequently denied a chance at the state finals. We knew that a rule was a rule, and we accepted that fate.
It has come to my attention that Rio Blanco High School has double standards when it comes to girls and boys athletics. Recently, a boy who failed classes repeatedly was passed on so that he would be able to compete in the regional tennis meet. I wish someone could explain to me how it is right that a repeat offender of the "no pass, no play' rule was passed so his partner would not have to play with someone he was not used to playing with and a first time offender (my original female partner) was turned away with a simple, "no." Furthermore, the boys' win-loss record does not equal the record my partner and I had two years ago.
I realize that the current boys double team would have a better chance of advancing to the state competition if the pairing was the same as always, but was not this the case two years ago? Should I infer that the girls did not have a good chance of making it to the state tournament and the boys do? Personally, I have to disagree with this assumption. The girls would have entered the regional meet undefeated and the current boys team has not achieved an accomplishment close to this.
I'm not questioning the "no pass, no play" rule, rather its equal application to all students. From my perspective, the rule is applied to only those who are not of the male gender. Several times, male athletes have been passed even though they did not earn it just so they would be able to play. If the rule is go-

ing to be compromised, why have the rule at all? If current school officials are not going to give equal treatment to all athletes and students, perhaps the Rio Blanco School District should appoint someone to this position who will.

*Sincerely,
Pamela Payne*

Discussion

1. Does it appear that there is a disparity in the way rules are handled between the boys and girls athletic teams? Explain your answer.
2. How should Rio Blanco officials respond to this letter? Who should respond?
3. What are some possible underlying reasons for allegedly "passing students on?"
4. Who should be involved if a formal inquiry is conducted into this matter?

Using School Facilities by Community Groups

Case

Marsha Martin, principal at Raging River High School, receives and approves requests for after-hours use of the building. For example, Pine Tree State University conducts a graduate-level program for teachers at RRHS as a service to the district's teachers. Ms. Martin, in fact, is a graduate of this PTSU program, and has never had any previous complaints from teachers where these graduate classes have been held. Historically, there have been no problems associated with any community group's usage of school's facilities.

Unfortunately, a series of complaints from Linda Long indicates that the PTSU group leaves her classroom in shambles. Ms. Long, a veteran teacher who is new to the district, claims that the graduate students alter the desk arrangement in her classroom and they refuse to replace the desks in their correct order when they leave. Linda further reports that supplies are missing from her desk, her overhead projector is damaged, and that the graduate students' food and drink messes pose potential hazards for her classroom computers.

Ms. Long says that the janitor, Ray Roberts, can verify the extent of these concerns. Linda requests that Ms. Martin deny building use to this group since they cannot control their members. Marsha wonders if Linda's loyalty to her cross-town alma mater, Riverside University, has any bearing on her recommendation.

Discussion

1. Is this a problem of management, regulation, or misplaced loyalty? Explain your answer.
2. Should Marsha Martin deny use of the building to community groups due to cleanup problems? Why or why not?
3. Who should Ms. Martin call to get advice on handling these matters?
4. List alternatives to denying use of the facility to the group.

Index
(by People Involved)

ASSISTANT PRINCIPALS

Addressing a Leaderless Campus, 3
Addressing Cafeteria Concerns, 4
Assessing Current Student Tardy Policies, 17
Changing from Teaching to Administrative Duties, 30
Compiling a Substitute Teachers' Handbook, 39
Disclosing Sensitive Issues, 59
Handling the Unauthorized Use of School Facilities, 85
Improving Student Attendance, 99
Observing Student-Initiated Segregation, 116
Regulating Participation in Extracurricular Activities, 138
Respecting the Assistant Principal, 145

AT-LARGE COMMUNITY

Banning Cell Phones in School, 28
Considering a Mandatory Drug Testing Program, 44
Defending Against Discrimination Accusations, 51
Determining Board Members' Political Agendas, 52
Eliminating Underclassman Hazing, 64

Grouping Grade Levels within a School District, 74
Handling a Crisis Situation, 77
Increasing Public Support of Education, 100
Mandating School Uniforms, 108
Merging Two Rival Schools, 110
Observing Student-Initiated Segregation, 116
Overemphasizing High School Football, 117
Praying at Football Games, 121
Revamping High School Graduation Ceremonies, 149
Reviewing an Open Campus Policy, 150
Treating Student Athletes Equally, 160
Using School Facilities by Community Groups, 162

AUXILIARY PERSONNEL

Accommodating Supplemental Instruction, 2
Addressing Cafeteria Concerns, 4
Assessing Building Climate, 15
Assessing Non-Custodial Parents' Rights, 18
Assessing School Office Decorum, 19
Assuring School Personnel Safety, 25
Cheating on the Test, 32

Index (by People Involved)

Controlling the Release of Students from School, 48
Determining Classified Personnel Job Descriptions, 53
Developing Special Educational Job Descriptions, 57
Evaluating Support Staff Performance, 69
Handling Common Transportation Problems, 81
Handling Complaints about Maintenance Personnel, 82
Impeding the School's Custodial Services, 94
Improving Campus Staff Teamwork, 96
Improving Custodial Services, 97
Managing Maintenance Personnel, 107
Mandating School Uniforms, 108
Merging Two Rival Schools, 110
Missing Curriculum Guides, 113
Preventing School Personnel From Using Others' Personal Materials, 129
Resolving Personality Conflicts, 144
Respecting the Assistant Principal, 145
Reviewing the Treasurer's Files, 152
Revising Teacher Observation Criteria, 156

CENTRAL OFFICE PERSONNEL

Accommodating Special Needs Students, 1
Addressing Secondary-Level Reading Problems, 10
Adopting a New Curricular Program, 11
Aligning District and Campus Personnel Roles, 12
Assigning Students to Achievement Groups, 23
Attending to Gifted Students' Needs, 27

Centralizing School Supplies, 29
Changing from Teaching to Administrative Duties, 30
Cheating on the Test, 32
Communicating Through Proper Channels, 35
Configuring Central Office Personnel Needs, 40
Confronting an Influential Booster Group, 42
Considering a New Budgeting Approach, 46
Dealing With an Ineffective Principal, 50
Determining Classified Personnel Job Descriptions, 53
Developing Special Educational Job Descriptions, 57
Disclosing Sensitive Issues, 59
Dismissing an Administrator, 60
Dueling Supervisory Authorities, 63
Extending Special Favors to School Board Members, 71
Grouping Grade Levels within a School District, 74
Handling Common Transportation Problems, 81
Handling Complaints about Maintenance Personnel, 82
Hiring a New Building Principal, 92
Improving Special Needs Students' Achievement Levels, 98
Initiating Supervisory Functions, 101
Maintaining Harmony Among Faculty, 104
Minimizing the Effects of a Transient Student Population, 112
Missing Curriculum Guides, 113
Prioritizing School Administrator Professional Development Activities, 130
Reviewing the Treasurer's Files, 152
Revising Teacher Transfer Policies, 157
Selecting New Textbooks, 159

Index (by People Involved) 165

COUNSELORS

Cheating on the Test, 32
Controlling Violence in a Special Education Classroom, 49
Reducing the Cost of Education, 137

PARENTS/GUARDIANS

Addressing Drug Problems, 8
Addressing Outside Recess Parameters, 9
Adopting a New Curricular Program, 11
Assessing Non-Custodial Parents' Rights, 18
Assigning Homework, 22
Attending Both Public and Private School Classes, 26
Attending to Gifted Students' Needs, 27
Banning Cell Phones in School, 28
Comparing Students' Efforts During a Parent-Teacher Conference, 37
Confronting an Influential Booster Group, 42
Considering a Mandatory Drug Testing Program, 44
Controlling the Release of Students from School, 48
Controlling Violence in a Special Education Classroom, 49
Defending Against Discrimination Accusations, 51
Determining Board Members' Political Agendas, 52
Determining Homework Accountability, 54
Determining Teacher Effectiveness, 55
Disclosing Sensitive Issues, 59
Eliminating Underclassman Hazing, 64
Enacting a Weapons Zero-Tolerance Policy, 66
Grouping Grade Levels within a School District, 74
Guarding Against Possible HIV Contamination, 76
Handling a Crisis Situation, 77
Handling a Split P.T.O., 79
Handling Common Transportation Problems, 81
Handling Student Discipline Problems, 83
Handling the Unauthorized Use of School Facilities, 85
Having Good Intentions but Setting a Bad Example, 90
Hiring a New Building Principal, 92
Improving Student Attendance, 99
Increasing Public Support of Education, 100
Locating a Missing Child, 103
Making Pupil Assignment Decisions, 106
Mandating School Uniforms, 108
Merging Two Rival Schools, 110
Minimizing Teaching Interruptions, 111
Overemphasizing High School Football, 117
Preparing for Parent-Teacher Conferences, 123
Rating Teachers on the Internet, 135
Removing a Bad Reputation, 140
Resolving Personality Conflicts, 144
Respecting the Confidentiality of Special Needs Students, 146
Revamping High School Graduation Ceremonies, 149
Reviewing an Open Campus Policy, 150

PRINCIPALS

Accommodating Special Needs Students, 1
Accommodating Supplemental Instruction, 2
Addressing a Leaderless Campus, 3
Addressing Cafeteria Concerns, 4

Index (by People Involved)

Addressing Drug Problems, 8
Addressing Outside Recess Parameters, 9
Addressing Secondary-Level Reading Problems, 10
Aligning District and Campus Personnel Roles, 12
Appraising a Family Member, 14
Assessing Building Climate, 15
Assessing Non-Custodial Parents' Rights, 18
Assessing School Office Decorum, 19
Assigning Homework, 22
Assigning Students to Achievement Groups, 23
Assuring School Personnel Safety, 25
Attending to Gifted Students' Needs, 27
Changing from Teaching to Administrative Duties, 30
Collecting Funds for Social Concerns, 34
Communicating Through Proper Channels, 35
Comparing Students' Efforts During a Parent-Teacher Conference, 37
Compiling a Substitute Teachers' Handbook, 39
Considering a New Budgeting Approach, 46
Controlling Library Censorship, 47
Controlling the Release of Students from School, 48
Controlling Violence in a Special Education Classroom, 49
Dealing With an Ineffective Principal, 50
Defending Against Discrimination Accusations, 51
Determining Classified Personnel Job Descriptions, 53
Developing a Safety Program, 56
Developing Classroom Management Expectations, 57
Disclosing Sensitive Issues, 59
Dismissing an Administrator, 60

Displaying Inappropriate Public Behavior, 61
Dueling Supervisory Authorities, 63
Enacting a Weapons Zero-Tolerance Policy, 66
Evaluating School Supply Procedures, 68
Evaluating Support Staff Performance, 69
Evaluating Teaching Effectiveness through Classroom Observations, 70
Grooming Standards for Student Teachers, 72
Grouping Grade Levels within a School District, 74
Guarding Against Possible HIV Contamination, 76
Handling a Crisis Situation, 77
Handling a Disruptive Student, 78
Handling a Split P.T.O., 79
Handling Common Transportation Problems, 81
Handling Complaints about Maintenance Personnel, 82
Handling Student Discipline Problems, 83
Handling the Unauthorized Use of School Facilities, 85
Harassing a Teacher: The Principal's Perspective, 86
Harassing a Teacher: The Teacher's Perspective, 88
Having Good Intentions but Setting a Bad Example, 90
Hiring a New Building Principal, 92
Impeding the School's Custodial Services, 94
Improving Campus Staff Teamwork, 96
Improving Custodial Services, 97
Initiating Supervisory Functions, 101
Locating a Missing Child, 103
Maintaining Harmony Among Faculty, 104
Managing Maintenance Personnel, 107
Mandating School Uniforms, 108

Index (by People Involved) 167

Mentoring New Teachers, 109
Merging Two Rival Schools, 110
Minimizing Teaching Interruptions, 111
Minimizing the Effects of a Transient Student Population, 112
Missing Curriculum Guides, 113
Monitoring Locker Rooms, 115
Observing Student-Initiated Segregation, 116
Overemphasizing High School Football, 117
Planning Effective Faculty Meetings, 118
Praying at Football Games, 121
Preventing School Personnel From Using Others' Personal Materials, 129
Prioritizing School Administrator Professional Development Activities, 130
Prioritizing Teacher Requests, 132
Promoting a Proposed Administrator Evaluation System, 133
Protecting Our Children, 134
Rating Teachers on the Internet, 135
Reducing the Cost of Education, 137
Regulating Participation in Extracurricular Activities, 138
Requiring Teachers to Perform Additional Duties, 143
Resolving Personality Conflicts, 144
Respecting the Assistant Principal, 145
Respecting the Confidentiality of Special Needs Students, 146
Revamping a Dysfunctional Grade-Level Team, 148
Revamping High School Graduation Ceremonies, 149
Reviewing an Open Campus Policy, 150
Revising Teacher Employment Applications, 154
Revising Teacher Observation Criteria, 156
Revising Teacher Transfer Policies, 157
Selecting High School Cheerleaders, 158

Using School Facilities by Community Groups, 162

SCHOOL BOARDS

Banning Cell Phones in School, 28
Changing from Teaching to Administrative Duties, 30
Considering a Mandatory Drug Testing Program, 44
Determining Board Members' Political Agendas, 52
Determining Homework Accountability, 54
Determining Teacher Effectiveness, 55
Dismissing an Administrator, 60
Displaying Inappropriate Public Behavior, 61
Enacting a Weapons Zero-Tolerance Policy, 66
Extending Special Favors to School Board Members, 71
Grouping Grade Levels within a School District, 74
Honoring a School Board Directive, 93
Increasing Public Support of Education, 100
Making Pupil Assignment Decisions, 106
Merging Two Rival Schools, 110
Overemphasizing High School Football, 117
Reducing the Cost of Education, 137
Requiring School District Residency, 142
Reviewing the Treasurer's Files, 152
Revising a Teacher Sick Leave Policy, 153

SPECIAL NEEDS PERSONNEL

Accommodating Special Needs Students, 1

Index (by People Involved)

Controlling Violence in a Special Education Classroom, 49
Developing Special Educational Job Descriptions, 57
Leaving a Special Education Classroom Unattended, 102
Respecting the Confidentiality of Special Needs Students, 146

STUDENTS

Accommodating Special Needs Students, 1
Addressing Cafeteria Concerns, 4
Addressing Drug Problems, 8
Aligning District and Campus Personnel Roles, 12
Assessing Current Student Tardy Policies, 17
Assessing Non-Custodial Parents' Rights, 18
Assessing School Office Decorum, 19
Assigning Homework, 22
Assigning Students to Achievement Groups, 23
Attending Both Public and Private School Classes, 26
Attending to Gifted Students' Needs, 27
Banning Cell Phones in School, 28
Cheating on the Test, 32
Considering a Mandatory Drug Testing Program, 44
Controlling Library Censorship, 47
Controlling the Release of Students from School, 48
Controlling Violence in a Special Education Classroom, 49
Defending Against Discrimination Accusations, 51
Determining Board Members' Political Agendas, 52
Determining Teacher Effectiveness, 55
Developing a Safety Program, 56

Developing Classroom Management Expectations, 57
Displaying Inappropriate Public Behavior, 61
Eliminating Underclassman Hazing, 64
Enacting a Weapons Zero-Tolerance Policy, 66
Evaluating Support Staff Performance, 69
Grouping Grade Levels within a School District, 74
Guarding Against Possible HIV Contamination, 76
Handling a Disruptive Student, 78
Handling Common Transportation Problems, 81
Handling Student Discipline Problems, 83
Having Good Intentions but Setting a Bad Example, 90
Improving Campus Staff Teamwork, 96
Improving Special Needs Students' Achievement Levels, 98
Improving Student Attendance, 99
Leaving a Special Education Classroom Unattended, 102
Locating a Missing Child, 103
Maintaining Harmony Among Faculty, 104
Making Pupil Assignment Decisions, 106
Mandating School Uniforms, 108
Merging Two Rival Schools, 110
Minimizing Teaching Interruptions, 111
Minimizing the Effects of a Transient Student Population, 112
Monitoring Locker Rooms, 115
Observing Student-Initiated Segregation, 116
Pledging to the American Flag, 120
Praying at Football Games, 121
Preventing Plagiarism, 125
Preventing Potential Internet Abuse, 127
Rating Teachers on the Internet, 135
Regulating Participation in Extracurricular Activities, 138

Index (by People Involved) 169

Removing a Bad Reputation, 140
Respecting the Assistant Principal, 145
Respecting the Confidentiality of Special Needs Students, 146
Revamping a Dysfunctional Grade-Level Team, 148
Revamping High School Graduation Ceremonies, 149
Reviewing an Open Campus Policy, 150
Selecting High School Cheerleaders, 158
Treating Student Athletes Equally, 160

SUPERINTENDENTS

Addressing a Leaderless Campus, 3
Addressing Drug Problems, 8
Aligning District and Campus Personnel Roles, 12
Attending Both Public and Private School Classes, 26
Communicating Through Proper Channels, 35
Configuring Central Office Personnel Needs, 40
Confronting an Influential Booster Group, 42
Considering a Mandatory Drug Testing Program, 44
Dealing With an Ineffective Principal, 50
Defending Against Discrimination Accusations, 51
Determining Board Members' Political Agendas, 52
Disclosing Sensitive Issues, 59
Dismissing an Administrator, 60
Displaying Inappropriate Public Behavior, 61
Eliminating Underclassman Hazing, 64
Extending Special Favors to School Board Members, 71

Grouping Grade Levels within a School District, 74
Handling a Crisis Situation, 77
Handling Common Transportation Problems, 81
Handling Complaints about Maintenance Personnel, 82
Harassing a Teacher: The Principal's Perspective, 86
Harassing a Teacher: The Teacher's Perspective, 88
Having Good Intentions but Setting a Bad Example, 90
Hiring a New Building Principal, 92
Honoring a School Board Directive, 93
Implementing a New Leadership Style, 95
Increasing Public Support of Education, 100
Overemphasizing High School Football, 117
Promoting a Proposed Administrator Evaluation System, 133
Reducing the Cost of Education, 137
Requiring School District Residency, 142
Revamping a Dysfunctional Grade-Level Team, 148
Reviewing the Treasurer's Files, 152
Revising a Teacher Sick Leave Policy, 153
Revising Teacher Transfer Policies, 157

TEACHERS

Accommodating Supplemental Instruction, 2
Addressing Curriculum Confusion, 6
Addressing Drug Problems, 8
Addressing Secondary-Level Reading Problems, 10
Adopting a New Curricular Program, 11
Aligning District and Campus Personnel Roles, 12

Index (by People Involved)

Appraising a Family Member, 14
Assessing Building Climate, 15
Assessing Current Student Tardy Policies, 17
Assessing Non-Custodial Parents' Rights, 18
Assessing the Legal Status of Student Teachers, 21
Assigning Homework, 22
Assigning Students to Achievement Groups, 23
Assuring School Personnel Safety, 25
Attending to Gifted Students' Needs, 27
Banning Cell Phones in School, 28
Changing from Teaching to Administrative Duties, 30
Collecting Funds for Social Concerns, 34
Comparing Students' Efforts During a Parent-Teacher Conference, 37
Configuring Central Office Personnel Needs, 40
Confronting an Influential Booster Group, 42
Considering a Mandatory Drug Testing Program, 44
Controlling Library Censorship, 47
Controlling Violence in a Special Education Classroom, 49
Dealing With an Ineffective Principal, 50
Determining Board Members' Political Agendas, 52
Determining Teacher Effectiveness, 55
Developing a Safety Program, 56
Developing Classroom Management Expectations, 57
Disclosing Sensitive Issues, 59
Dismissing an Administrator, 60
Dueling Supervisory Authorities, 63
Evaluating School Supply Procedures, 68
Evaluating Support Staff Performance, 69

Evaluating Teaching Effectiveness through Classroom Observations, 70
Grooming Standards for Student Teachers, 72
Grouping Grade Levels within a School District, 74
Guarding Against Possible HIV Contamination, 76
Handling Student Discipline Problems, 83
Handling the Unauthorized Use of School Facilities, 85
Harassing a Teacher: The Principal's Perspective, 86
Harassing a Teacher: The Teacher's Perspective, 88
Hiring a New Building Principal, 92
Impeding the School's Custodial Services, 94
Improving Campus Staff Teamwork, 96
Improving Special Needs Students' Achievement Levels, 98
Improving Student Attendance, 99
Initiating Supervisory Functions, 101
Leaving a Special Education Classroom Unattended, 102
Maintaining Harmony Among Faculty, 104
Managing Maintenance Personnel, 107
Mandating School Uniforms, 108
Mentoring New Teachers, 109
Merging Two Rival Schools, 110
Minimizing Teaching Interruptions, 111
Minimizing the Effects of a Transient Student Population, 112
Missing Curriculum Guides, 113
Monitoring Locker Rooms, 115
Overemphasizing High School Football, 117
Planning Effective Faculty Meetings, 118
Pledging to the American Flag, 120
Preparing an Integrated Instructional Unit, 122
Preparing for Parent-Teacher Conferences, 123

Preventing Plagiarism, 125
Preventing Potential Internet Abuse, 127
Preventing School Personnel From Using Others' Personal Materials, 129
Prioritizing Teacher Requests, 132
Protecting Our Children, 134
Rating Teachers on the Internet, 135
Reducing the Cost of Education, 137
Removing a Bad Reputation, 140
Requiring School District Residency, 142
Requiring Teachers to Perform Additional Duties, 143
Resolving Personality Conflicts, 144
Respecting the Assistant Principal, 145
Revamping a Dysfunctional Grade-Level Team, 148
Revamping High School Graduation Ceremonies, 149
Revising a Teacher Sick Leave Policy, 153
Revising Teacher Employment Applications, 154
Revising Teacher Transfer Policies, 157
Selecting New Textbooks, 159
Using School Facilities by Community Groups, 162

Index
(by Sites)

DISTRICT-LEVEL

Accommodating Special Needs Students, 1
Addressing Cafeteria Concerns, 4
Addressing Secondary-Level Reading Problems, 10
Adopting a New Curricular Program, 11
Aligning District and Campus Personnel Roles, 12
Attending to Gifted Students' Needs, 27
Banning Cell Phones in School, 28
Centralizing School Supplies, 29
Communicating Through Proper Channels, 35
Configuring Central Office Personnel Needs, 40
Considering a Mandatory Drug Testing Program, 44
Considering a New Budgeting Approach, 46
Determining Board Members' Political Agendas, 52
Determining Classified Personnel Job Descriptions, 53
Determining Teacher Effectiveness, 55
Developing Special Educational Job Descriptions, 58
Disclosing Sensitive Issues, 59
Dismissing an Administrator, 60
Extending Special Favors to School Board Members, 71
Grouping Grade Levels within a School District, 74
Handling Common Transportation Problems, 81
Handling Complaints about Maintenance Personnel, 82
Honoring a School Board Directive, 93
Implementing a New Leadership Style, 95
Improving Special Needs Students' Achievement Levels, 98
Increasing Public Support of Education, 100
Initiating Supervisory Functions, 101
Prioritizing School Administrator Professional Development Activities, 130
Promoting a Proposed Administrator Evaluation System, 133
Reducing the Cost of Education, 137
Requiring School District Residency, 142
Reviewing the Treasurer's Files, 152
Revising a Teacher Sick Leave Policy, 153
Revising Teacher Employment Applications, 154
Revising Teacher Transfer Policies, 157
Selecting New Textbooks, 159

ELEMENTARY-LEVEL SCHOOLS

Accommodating Special Needs Students, 1
Accommodating Supplemental Instruction, 2
Addressing Curriculum Confusion, 6
Addressing Outside Recess Parameters, 9
Aligning District and Campus Personnel Roles, 12
Assessing Building Climate, 15
Assessing Non-Custodial Parents' Rights, 18
Assigning Homework, 22
Assigning Students to Achievement Groups, 23
Changing from Teaching to Administrative Duties, 30
Comparing Students' Efforts During a Parent-Teacher Conference, 37
Considering a New Budgeting Approach, 46
Controlling the Release of Students from School, 48
Controlling Violence in a Special Education Classroom, 49
Defending Against Discrimination Accusations, 51
Determining Classified Personnel Job Descriptions, 53
Developing a Safety Program, 56
Displaying Inappropriate Public Behavior, 61
Dueling Supervisory Authorities, 63
Evaluating School Supply Procedures, 68
Evaluating Teaching Effectiveness through Classroom Observations, 70
Grouping Grade Levels within a School District, 74
Handling a Disruptive Student, 78
Handling a Split P.T.O., 79
Handling Student Discipline Problems, 83
Harassing a Teacher: The Principal's Perspective, 86
Harassing a Teacher: The Teacher's Perspective, 88
Having Good Intentions but Setting a Bad Example, 90
Hiring a New Building Principal, 92
Honoring a School Board Directive, 93
Impeding the School's Custodial Services, 94
Improving Custodial Services, 97
Locating a Missing Child, 103
Making Pupil Assignment Decisions, 106
Managing Maintenance Personnel, 107
Mandating School Uniforms, 108
Mentoring New Teachers, 109
Missing Curriculum Guides, 113
Observing Student-Initiated Segregation, 116
Pledging to the American Flag, 120
Preparing for Parent-Teacher Conferences, 123
Prioritizing School Administrator Professional Development Activities, 130
Prioritizing Teacher Requests, 132
Respecting the Confidentiality of Special Needs Students, 146
Revising Teacher Employment Applications, 154

HIGH SCHOOLS

Addressing a Leaderless Campus, 3
Addressing Drug Problems, 8
Addressing Secondary-Level Reading Problems, 10
Appraising a Family Member, 14
Assessing Current Student Tardy Policies, 17
Assessing School Office Decorum, 19
Attending Both Public and Private School Classes, 26

Index (by Sites)

Banning Cell Phones in School, 28
Cheating on the Test, 32
Collecting Funds for Social Concerns, 34
Compiling a Substitute Teachers' Handbook, 39
Confronting an Influential Booster Group, 42
Controlling Library Censorship, 47
Eliminating Underclassman Hazing, 64
Enacting a Weapons Zero-Tolerance Policy, 66
Grooming Standards for Student Teachers, 72
Grouping Grade Levels within a School District, 74
Guarding Against Possible HIV Contamination, 76
Handling a Crisis Situation, 77
Honoring a School Board Directive, 93
Improving Campus Staff Teamwork, 96
Leaving a Special Education Classroom Unattended, 102
Making Pupil Assignment Decisions, 106
Overemphasizing High School Football, 117
Praying at Football Games, 121
Preventing Plagiarism, 125
Preventing Potential Internet Abuse, 127
Preventing School Personnel From Using Others' Personal Materials, 129
Prioritizing School Administrator Professional Development Activities, 130
Protecting Our Children, 134
Rating Teachers on the Internet, 135
Regulating Participation in Extracurricular Activities, 138
Removing a Bad Reputation, 140
Requiring Teachers to Perform Additional Duties, 143
Revamping High School Graduation Ceremonies, 149
Reviewing an Open Campus Policy, 150
Revising Teacher Observation Criteria, 156
Selecting High School Cheerleaders, 158
Selecting New Textbooks, 159
Treating Student Athletes Equally, 160
Using School Facilities by Community Groups, 162

MIDDLE SCHOOLS / JUNIOR HIGH SCHOOLS

Addressing Cafeteria Concerns, 4
Aligning District and Campus Personnel Roles, 12
Assessing the Legal Status of Student Teachers, 21
Dealing With an Ineffective Principal, 50
Determining Homework Accountability, 54
Developing Classroom Management Expectations, 57
Evaluating Support Staff Performance, 69
Grouping Grade Levels within a School District, 74
Handling Common Transportation Problems, 81
Handling the Unauthorized Use of School Facilities, 85
Honoring a School Board Directive, 93
Improving Student Attendance, 99
Maintaining Harmony Among Faculty, 104
Merging Two Rival Schools, 110
Minimizing Teaching Interruptions, 111
Minimizing the Effects of a Transient Student Population, 112
Monitoring Locker Rooms, 115
Planning Effective Faculty Meetings, 118

Preparing an Integrated Instructional Unit, 122
Prioritizing School Administrator Professional Development Activities, 130
Protecting Our Children, 134
Resolving Personality Conflicts, 144
Respecting the Assistant Principal, 145
Revamping a Dysfunctional Grade-Level Team, 148
Reviewing an Open Campus Policy, 150
Selecting New Textbooks, 159

Index
(by Topics)

ACCOUNTABILITY

Accommodating Supplemental Instruction, 2
Addressing Secondary-Level Reading Problems, 10
Adopting a New Curricular Program, 11
Assigning Students to Achievement Groups, 23
Cheating on the Test, 32
Comparing Students' Efforts During a Parent-Teacher Conference, 37
Configuring Central Office Personnel Needs, 40
Considering a Mandatory Drug Testing Program, 44
Considering a New Budgeting Approach, 46
Determining Homework Accountability, 54
Determining Teacher Effectiveness, 55
Developing Classroom Management Expectations, 57
Evaluating Teaching Effectiveness through Classroom Observations, 70
Grouping Grade Levels within a School District, 74
Improving Special Needs Students' Achievement Levels, 98
Improving Student Attendance, 99
Initiating Supervisory Functions, 101
Maintaining Harmony Among Faculty, 104
Making Pupil Assignment Decisions, 106
Minimizing Teaching Interruptions, 111
Minimizing the Effects of a Transient Student Population, 112
Missing Curriculum Guides, 113
Preparing an Integrated Instructional Unit, 122
Preparing for Parent-Teacher Conferences, 123
Prioritizing School Administrator Professional Development Activities, 130
Promoting a Proposed Administrator Evaluation System, 133
Reducing the Cost of Education, 137
Removing a Bad Reputation, 140
Revising Teacher Observation Criteria, 156
Selecting New Textbooks, 159

CLIMATE

Accommodating Special Needs Students, 1
Addressing a Leaderless Campus, 3
Addressing Cafeteria Concerns, 4
Addressing Curriculum Confusion, 6
Addressing Drug Problems, 8
Aligning District and Campus Personnel Roles, 12

Index (by Topics)

Appraising a Family Member, 14
Assessing Building Climate, 15
Assessing Current Student Tardy Policies, 17
Assessing Non-Custodial Parents' Rights, 18
Assessing School Office Decorum, 19
Assuring School Personnel Safety, 25
Banning Cell Phones in School, 28
Changing from Teaching to Administrative Duties, 30
Collecting Funds for Social Concerns, 34
Communicating Through Proper Channels, 35
Comparing Students' Efforts During a Parent-Teacher Conference, 37
Compiling a Substitute Teachers Handbook, 39
Configuring Central Office Personnel Needs, 40
Confronting an Influential Booster Group, 42
Considering a New Budgeting Approach, 46
Dealing With an Ineffective Principal, 50
Defending Against Discrimination Accusations, 51
Determining Board Members' Political Agendas, 52
Determining Classified Personnel Job Descriptions, 53
Developing a Safety Program, 56
Developing Classroom Management Expectations, 57
Developing Special Educational Job Descriptions, 58
Dismissing an Administrator, 60
Displaying Inappropriate Public Behavior, 61
Enacting a Weapons Zero-Tolerance Policy, 66
Evaluating School Supply Procedures, 68

Evaluating Support Staff Performance, 69
Evaluating Teaching Effectiveness through Classroom Observations, 70
Grooming Standards for Student Teachers, 72
Grouping Grade Levels within a School District, 74
Guarding Against Possible HIV Contamination, 76
Handling a Crisis Situation, 77
Handling a Disruptive Student, 78
Handling a Split P.T.O., 79
Handling Complaints about Maintenance Personnel, 82
Handling Student Discipline Problems, 83
Harassing a Teacher: The Principal's Perspective, 86
Harassing a Teacher: The Teacher's Perspective, 88
Having Good Intentions but Setting a Bad Example, 90
Honoring a School Board Directive, 93
Impeding the School's Custodial Services, 94
Implementing a New Leadership Style, 95
Improving Campus Staff Teamwork, 96
Improving Custodial Services, 97
Improving Student Attendance, 99
Initiating Supervisory Functions, 101
Maintaining Harmony Among Faculty, 104
Managing Maintenance Personnel, 107
Mandating School Uniforms, 108
Mentoring New Teachers, 109
Merging Two Rival Schools, 110
Minimizing Teaching Interruptions, 111
Minimizing the Effects of a Transient Student Population, 112
Missing Curriculum Guides, 113
Observing Student-Initiated Segregation, 116

Index (by Topics)   179

Planning Effective Faculty Meetings, 118
Preparing for Parent-Teacher Conferences, 123
Preventing Plagiarism, 125
Preventing School Personnel From Using Others' Personal Materials, 129
Prioritizing School Administrator Professional Development Activities, 130
Prioritizing Teacher Requests, 132
Promoting a Proposed Administrator Evaluation System, 133
Protecting Our Children, 134
Reducing the Cost of Education, 137
Removing a Bad Reputation, 140
Requiring Teachers to Perform Additional Duties, 143
Resolving Personality Conflicts, 144
Respecting the Assistant Principal, 145
Revamping a Dysfunctional Grade-Level Team, 148
Revising a Teacher Sick Leave Policy, 153
Revising Teacher Observation Criteria, 156
Revising Teacher Transfer Policies, 157
Selecting New Textbooks, 159
Using School Facilities by Community Groups, 162

COMMUNICATION

Accommodating Special Needs Students, 1
Accommodating Supplemental Instruction, 2
Addressing a Leaderless Campus, 3
Addressing Outside Recess Parameters, 9
Assessing Non-Custodial Parents' Rights, 18
Assessing School Office Decorum, 19
Assessing the Legal Status of Student Teachers, 21
Assigning Students to Achievement Groups, 23
Assuring School Personnel Safety, 25
Attending to Gifted Students' Needs, 27
Banning Cell Phones in School, 28
Centralizing School Supplies, 29
Changing from Teaching to Administrative Duties, 30
Cheating on the Test, 32
Communicating Through Proper Channels, 35
Comparing Students' Efforts During a Parent-Teacher Conference, 37
Compiling a Substitute Teachers Handbook, 39
Confronting an Influential Booster Group, 42
Considering a New Budgeting Approach, 46
Controlling the Release of Students from School, 48
Dealing With an Ineffective Principal, 50
Defending Against Discrimination Accusations, 51
Determining Board Members' Political Agendas, 52
Determining Classified Personnel Job Descriptions, 53
Determining Homework Accountability, 54
Determining Teacher Effectiveness, 55
Disclosing Sensitive Issues, 59
Displaying Inappropriate Public Behavior, 61
Dueling Supervisory Authorities, 63
Eliminating Underclassman Hazing, 64
Evaluating School Supply Procedures, 68
Evaluating Teaching Effectiveness through Classroom Observations, 70
Extending Special Favors to School Board Members, 71

Index (by Topics)

Grooming Standards for Student Teachers, 72
Guarding Against Possible HIV Contamination, 76
Handling a Crisis Situation, 77
Handling a Split P.T.O., 79
Handling Common Transportation Problems, 81
Handling Complaints about Maintenance Personnel, 82
Handling the Unauthorized Use of School Facilities, 85
Having Good Intentions but Setting a Bad Example, 90
Hiring a New Building Principal, 92
Honoring a School Board Directive, 93
Impeding the School's Custodial Services, 94
Implementing a New Leadership Style, 95
Improving Campus Staff Teamwork, 96
Improving Custodial Services, 97
Improving Student Attendance, 99
Increasing Public Support of Education, 100
Initiating Supervisory Functions, 101
Locating a Missing Child, 103
Making Pupil Assignment Decisions, 106
Managing Maintenance Personnel, 107
Mentoring New Teachers, 109
Merging Two Rival Schools, 110
Planning Effective Faculty Meetings, 118
Preparing for Parent-Teacher Conferences, 123
Preventing Plagiarism, 125
Preventing Potential Internet Abuse, 127
Preventing School Personnel From Using Others' Personal Materials, 129
Prioritizing School Administrator Professional Development Activities, 130
Promoting a Proposed Administrator Evaluation System, 133
Protecting Our Children, 134

Removing a Bad Reputation, 140
Resolving Personality Conflicts, 144
Respecting the Assistant Principal, 145
Respecting the Confidentiality of Special Needs Students, 146
Revamping a Dysfunctional Grade-Level Team, 148
Revamping High School Graduation Ceremonies, 149
Revising Teacher Transfer Policies, 157
Selecting New Textbooks, 159
Treating Student Athletes Equally, 160
Using School Facilities by Community Groups, 162

CONFLICT MANAGEMENT

Accommodating Supplemental Instruction, 2
Addressing a Leaderless Campus, 3
Addressing Curriculum Confusion, 6
Adopting a New Curricular Program, 11
Assessing Building Climate, 15
Assessing Non-Custodial Parents' Rights, 18
Assessing the Legal Status of Student Teachers, 21
Assigning Students to Achievement Groups, 23
Assuring School Personnel Safety, 25
Attending Both Public and Private School Classes, 26
Attending to Gifted Students' Needs, 27
Banning Cell Phones in School, 28
Changing from Teaching to Administrative Duties, 30
Cheating on the Test, 32
Communicating Through Proper Channels, 35
Comparing Students' Efforts During a Parent-Teacher Conference, 37
Configuring Central Office Personnel Needs, 40

Confronting an Influential Booster Group, 42
Considering a New Budgeting Approach, 46
Controlling Library Censorship, 47
Controlling the Release of Students from School, 48
Dealing With an Ineffective Principal, 50
Defending Against Discrimination Accusations, 51
Determining Board Members' Political Agendas, 52
Determining Classified Personnel Job Descriptions, 53
Determining Homework Accountability, 54
Developing Special Educational Job Descriptions, 58
Disclosing Sensitive Issues, 59
Dismissing an Administrator, 60
Displaying Inappropriate Public Behavior, 61
Dueling Supervisory Authorities, 63
Eliminating Underclassman Hazing, 64
Enacting a Weapons Zero-Tolerance Policy, 66
Evaluating Support Staff Performance, 69
Evaluating Teaching Effectiveness through Classroom Observations, 70
Grooming Standards for Student Teachers, 72
Grouping Grade Levels within a School District, 74
Guarding Against Possible HIV Contamination, 76
Handling a Crisis Situation, 77
Handling a Split P.T.O., 79
Handling Common Transportation Problems, 81
Handling Student Discipline Problems, 83
Handling the Unauthorized Use of School Facilities, 85

Harassing a Teacher: The Principal's Perspective, 86
Harassing a Teacher: The Teacher's Perspective, 88
Having Good Intentions but Setting a Bad Example, 90
Honoring a School Board Directive, 93
Implementing a New Leadership Style, 95
Improving Campus Staff Teamwork, 96
Leaving a Special Education Classroom Unattended, 102
Locating a Missing Child, 103
Maintaining Harmony Among Faculty, 104
Making Pupil Assignment Decisions, 106
Managing Maintenance Personnel, 107
Mandating School Uniforms, 108
Mentoring New Teachers, 109
Merging Two Rival Schools, 110
Minimizing Teaching Interruptions, 111
Overemphasizing High School Football, 117
Planning Effective Faculty Meetings, 118
Pledging to the American Flag, 120
Praying at Football Games, 121
Preparing for Parent-Teacher Conferences, 123
Preventing Plagiarism, 125
Preventing School Personnel From Using Others' Personal Materials, 129
Prioritizing School Administrator Professional Development Activities, 130
Promoting a Proposed Administrator Evaluation System, 133
Protecting Our Children, 134
Reducing the Cost of Education, 137
Removing a Bad Reputation, 140
Requiring Teachers to Perform Additional Duties, 143
Resolving Personality Conflicts, 144

Respecting the Assistant Principal, 145
Respecting the Confidentiality of Special Needs Students, 146
Revamping a Dysfunctional Grade-Level Team, 148
Revamping High School Graduation Ceremonies, 149
Reviewing an Open Campus Policy, 150
Revising Teacher Observation Criteria, 156
Revising Teacher Transfer Policies, 157
Selecting High School Cheerleaders, 158
Selecting New Textbooks, 159
Treating Student Athletes Equally, 160
Using School Facilities by Community Groups, 162

CURRICULUM

Accommodating Special Needs Students, 1
Accommodating Supplemental Instruction, 2
Addressing Curriculum Confusion, 6
Addressing Secondary-Level Reading Problems, 10
Adopting a New Curricular Program, 11
Assessing Current Student Tardy Policies, 17
Assigning Homework, 22
Assigning Students to Achievement Groups, 23
Attending Both Public and Private School Classes, 26
Attending to Gifted Students' Needs, 27
Comparing Students' Efforts During a Parent-Teacher Conference, 37
Configuring Central Office Personnel Needs, 40
Considering a New Budgeting Approach, 46
Controlling Library Censorship, 47
Determining Homework Accountability, 54

Developing a Safety Program, 56
Developing Classroom Management Expectations, 57
Evaluating Teaching Effectiveness through Classroom Observations, 70
Grouping Grade Levels within a School District, 74
Honoring a School Board Directive, 93
Improving Special Needs Students' Achievement Levels, 98
Maintaining Harmony Among Faculty, 104
Mentoring New Teachers, 109
Merging Two Rival Schools, 110
Minimizing Teaching Interruptions, 111
Minimizing the Effects of a Transient Student Population, 112
Missing Curriculum Guides, 113
Preparing an Integrated Instructional Unit, 122
Preparing for Parent-Teacher Conferences, 123
Preventing Plagiarism, 125
Prioritizing School Administrator Professional Development Activities, 130
Prioritizing Teacher Requests, 132
Rating Teachers on the Internet, 135
Reducing the Cost of Education, 137
Regulating Participation in Extracurricular Activities, 138
Removing a Bad Reputation, 140
Revamping a Dysfunctional Grade-Level Team, 148
Revising Teacher Observation Criteria, 156
Selecting New Textbooks, 159

DIVERSITY

Accommodating Special Needs Students, 1
Addressing Curriculum Confusion, 6

Index (by Topics) 183

Addressing Secondary-Level Reading Problems, 10
Adopting a New Curricular Program, 11
Assessing Building Climate, 15
Assessing Non-Custodial Parents' Rights, 18
Assessing the Legal Status of Student Teachers, 21
Attending Both Public and Private School Classes, 26
Attending to Gifted Students' Needs, 27
Changing from Teaching to Administrative Duties, 30
Collecting Funds for Social Concerns, 32
Controlling Library Censorship, 47
Controlling the Release of Students from School, 48
Controlling Violence in a Special Education Classroom, 49
Defending Against Discrimination Accusations, 51
Developing Special Educational Job Descriptions, 58
Displaying Inappropriate Public Behavior, 61
Grooming Standards for Student Teachers, 72
Guarding Against Possible HIV Contamination, 76
Improving Special Needs Students' Achievement Levels, 98
Leaving a Special Education Classroom Unattended, 102
Maintaining Harmony Among Faculty, 104
Mandating School Uniforms, 108
Minimizing the Effects of a Transient Student Population, 112
Observing Student-Initiated Segregation, 116
Pledging to the American Flag, 120
Praying at Football Games, 121
Prioritizing School Administrator Professional Development Activities, 130

Prioritizing Teacher Requests, 132
Regulating Participation in Extracurricular Activities, 138
Removing a Bad Reputation, 140
Respecting the Confidentiality of Special Needs Students, 146
Revamping High School Graduation Ceremonies, 149
Revising Teacher Employment Applications, 154

ETHICS

Addressing a Leaderless Campus, 3
Addressing Curriculum Confusion, 6
Addressing Drug Problems, 8
Appraising a Family Member, 14
Assessing Non-Custodial Parents' Rights, 18
Assuring School Personnel Safety, 25
Attending Both Public and Private School Classes, 26
Banning Cell Phones in School, 28
Changing from Teaching to Administrative Duties, 30
Cheating on the Test, 32
Collecting Funds for Social Concerns, 34
Communicating Through Proper Channels, 35
Comparing Students' Efforts During a Parent-Teacher Conference, 37
Confronting an Influential Booster Group, 42
Considering a Mandatory Drug Testing Program, 44
Controlling the Release of Students from School, 48
Dealing With an Ineffective Principal, 50
Defending Against Discrimination Accusations, 51
Determining Board Members' Political Agendas, 52

Determining Teacher Effectiveness, 55
Developing a Safety Program, 56
Developing Special Educational Job Descriptions, 58
Dismissing an Administrator, 60
Displaying Inappropriate Public Behavior, 61
Enacting a Weapons Zero-Tolerance Policy, 66
Evaluating Teaching Effectiveness through Classroom Observations, 70
Grooming Standards for Student Teachers, 72
Guarding Against Possible HIV Contamination, 76
Handling a Disruptive Student, 78
Harassing a Teacher: The Principal's Perspective, 86
Harassing a Teacher: The Teacher's Perspective, 88
Having Good Intentions but Setting a Bad Example, 90
Implementing a New Leadership Style, 95
Improving Special Needs Students' Achievement Levels, 98
Mandating School Uniforms, 108
Minimizing the Effects of a Transient Student Population, 112
Observing Student-Initiated Segregation, 116
Pledging to the American Flag, 120
Praying at Football Games, 121
Preventing Plagiarism, 125
Preventing School Personnel From Using Others' Personal Materials, 129
Prioritizing School Administrator Professional Development Activities, 130
Prioritizing Teacher Requests, 132
Promoting a Proposed Administrator Evaluation System, 133
Protecting Our Children, 134
Rating Teachers on the Internet, 135

Reducing the Cost of Education, 137
Removing a Bad Reputation, 140
Requiring School District Residency, 142
Requiring Teachers to Perform Additional Duties, 143
Resolving Personality Conflicts, 144
Respecting the Assistant Principal, 145
Revamping a Dysfunctional Grade-Level Team, 148
Reviewing an Open Campus Policy, 150
Revising a Teacher Sick Leave Policy, 153
Revising Teacher Transfer Policies, 157
Treating Student Athletes Equally, 160

LEGAL

Accommodating Special Needs Students, 1
Addressing a Leaderless Campus, 3
Addressing Curriculum Confusion, 6
Addressing Drug Problems, 8
Assessing Non-Custodial Parents' Rights, 18
Assessing the Legal Status of Student Teachers, 21
Assuring School Personnel Safety, 25
Attending Both Public and Private School Classes, 26
Banning Cell Phones in School, 28
Cheating on the Test, 32
Collecting Funds for Social Concerns, 34
Comparing Students' Efforts During a Parent-Teacher Conference, 37
Confronting an Influential Booster Group, 42
Considering a Mandatory Drug Testing Program, 44
Controlling the Release of Students from School, 48
Controlling Violence in a Special Education Classroom, 49

Index (by Topics) 185

Dealing With an Ineffective Principal, 50
Defending Against Discrimination Accusations, 51
Determining Classified Personnel Job Descriptions, 53
Determining Homework Accountability, 54
Determining Teacher Effectiveness, 55
Developing Special Educational Job Descriptions, 58
Disclosing Sensitive Issues, 59
Dismissing an Administrator, 60
Displaying Inappropriate Public Behavior, 61
Eliminating Underclassman Hazing, 64
Enacting a Weapons Zero-Tolerance Policy, 66
Evaluating Support Staff Performance, 69
Evaluating Teaching Effectiveness through Classroom Observations, 70
Extending Special Favors to School Board Members, 71
Grooming Standards for Student Teachers, 72
Guarding Against Possible HIV Contamination, 76
Handling a Crisis Situation, 77
Handling a Disruptive Student, 78
Handling Common Transportation Problems, 81
Handling the Unauthorized Use of School Facilities, 85
Harassing a Teacher: The Principal's Perspective, 86
Harassing a Teacher: The Teacher's Perspective, 88
Having Good Intentions but Setting a Bad Example, 90
Hiring a New Building Principal, 92
Honoring a School Board Directive, 93
Improving Special Needs Students' Achievement Levels, 98
Improving Student Attendance, 99

Leaving a Special Education Classroom Unattended, 102
Locating a Missing Child, 103
Making Pupil Assignment Decisions, 106
Mandating School Uniforms, 108
Minimizing Teaching Interruptions, 111
Monitoring Locker Rooms, 115
Pledging to the American Flag, 120
Praying at Football Games, 121
Preparing an Integrated Instructional Unit, 122
Preventing Plagiarism, 125
Preventing Potential Internet Abuse, 127
Prioritizing School Administrator Professional Development Activities, 130
Prioritizing Teacher Requests, 132
Promoting a Proposed Administrator Evaluation System, 133
Protecting Our Children, 134
Rating Teachers on the Internet, 135
Reducing the Cost of Education, 137
Requiring School District Residency, 142
Requiring Teachers to Perform Additional Duties, 143
Respecting the Assistant Principal, 145
Respecting the Confidentiality of Special Needs Students, 146
Reviewing the Treasurer's Files, 152
Revising a Teacher Sick Leave Policy, 153
Revising Teacher Employment Applications, 154
Revising Teacher Observation Criteria, 156
Revising Teacher Transfer Policies, 157
Treating Student Athletes Equally, 160

POLITICS

Addressing Curriculum Confusion, 6
Addressing Drug Problems, 8

Index (by Topics)

Adopting a New Curricular Program, 11
Appraising a Family Member, 14
Assessing Building Climate, 15
Assessing Non-Custodial Parents' Rights, 18
Assessing School Office Decorum, 19
Attending Both Public and Private School Classes, 26
Attending to Gifted Students' Needs, 27
Banning Cell Phones in School, 28
Changing from Teaching to Administrative Duties, 30
Communicating Through Proper Channels, 35
Comparing Students' Efforts During a Parent-Teacher Conference, 38
Configuring Central Office Personnel Needs, 40
Confronting an Influential Booster Group, 42
Considering a Mandatory Drug Testing Program, 44
Controlling Library Censorship, 47
Dealing With an Ineffective Principal, 50
Defending Against Discrimination Accusations, 51
Determining Board Members' Political Agendas, 52
Developing Special Educational Job Descriptions, 58
Disclosing Sensitive Issues, 59
Dismissing an Administrator, 60
Displaying Inappropriate Public Behavior, 61
Dueling Supervisory Authorities, 63
Enacting a Weapons Zero-Tolerance Policy, 66
Extending Special Favors to School Board Members, 71
Grouping Grade Levels within a School District, 74
Guarding Against Possible HIV Contamination, 76
Handling a Crisis Situation, 77
Handling a Split P.T.O., 79
Handling Complaints about Maintenance Personnel, 82
Handling Student Discipline Problems, 83
Handling the Unauthorized Use of School Facilities, 85
Harassing a Teacher: The Principal's Perspective, 86
Harassing a Teacher: The Teacher's Perspective, 88
Having Good Intentions but Setting a Bad Example, 90
Hiring a New Building Principal, 92
Honoring a School Board Directive, 93
Implementing a New Leadership Style, 95
Improving Custodial Services, 97
Improving Special Needs Students' Achievement Levels, 98
Increasing Public Support of Education, 100
Maintaining Harmony Among Faculty, 104
Mandating School Uniforms, 108
Merging Two Rival Schools, 110
Minimizing Teaching Interruptions, 111
Observing Student-Initiated Segregation, 116
Overemphasizing High School Football, 117
Pledging to the American Flag, 120
Praying at Football Games, 121
Preparing an Integrated Instructional Unit, 122
Preventing Plagiarism, 125
Prioritizing School Administrator Professional Development Activities, 130
Prioritizing Teacher Requests, 132
Promoting a Proposed Administrator Evaluation System, 133
Protecting Our Children, 134
Reducing the Cost of Education, 137

Removing a Bad Reputation, 140
Requiring School District Residency, 142
Resolving Personality Conflicts, 144
Respecting the Assistant Principal, 145
Revamping a Dysfunctional Grade-Level Team, 148
Revamping High School Graduation Ceremonies, 149
Reviewing an Open Campus Policy, 150
Reviewing the Treasurer's Files, 152
Revising Teacher Observation Criteria, 156
Revising Teacher Transfer Policies, 157
Selecting High School Cheerleaders, 158
Selecting New Textbooks, 159
Treating Student Athletes Equally, 160
Using School Facilities by Community Groups, 162

TECHNOLOGY

Banning Cell Phones in School, 28
Minimizing Teaching Interruptions, 111
Preventing Plagiarism, 125
Preventing Potential Internet Abuse, 127
Prioritizing School Administrator Professional Development Activities, 130
Rating Teachers on the Internet, 135